Peppino D'Agostino's New Acoustic Guitar

Special Thanks

I want to thank all the people who knowingly and unknowingly helped make this book possible, including Aaron Stang and everybody at Warner Bros. Publications; Dylan Schorer for his patience, precision and ability in transcribing my music; Robert Godin, Katherine Calder, Brian McConnell and everybody at the Godin Guitar Company; George Nauful and Jim Snowden at Mesa Blue Moon Records; Lloyd Baggs for his friendship and for setting a new standard in acoustic amplification systems; Rob Griffin for his brilliant engineering; my wife Donna and my daughter Aleza for their love and support; Alfredo Morabito in Rome; my Family and Friends in Italy; all my guitar heroes for their inspiration; my guitar students who make me reflect about music, and Corrado Rustici for his encouragement. A special thanks goes to the Muse of Music which keeps visiting me and tapping very lightly on my shoulders during all the long hours in my studio.

Transcribed by: Dylan Schorer and Peppino D'Agostino

Project Manager/Editor: Aaron Stang
Cover Design: Joseph Klucar
Engraving: Dylan Schorer
Technical Editors: Glyn Dryhurst & Dale Sloman
Photography: Cathy Rath

Introduction

The majority of the exercises, arrangements, and original compositions in the book were inspired and written utilizing various open tunings. When using an open tuning, all the chords and scales are found in different and unfamiliar positions on the fretboard. The reason we're using tablature in addition to the conventional music notation, is because the changed location of the notes, caused by the different open tunings, makes playing from common music notation extremely difficult. The majority of players and students interested in experimenting with open tunings, play by referring mainly to tablature, and use traditional music notation to understand the rhythmic structure and harmonic content of the song.

The book is divided into 7 different tunings. In each section (except the one in the standard EADGBE tuning), you'll find a segment that explains how to tune your guitar from standard tuning to the chosen open tuning, a chord chart to become familiar with the new location of different chords on the fretboard, a short exercise, a brief arrangement of a well known piece, and finally, at least one of my original compositions.

We've tried very hard to be as accurate and informative as possible. The right and left hand fingering is on the music staff, and both the chord names and chord diagrams are shown.

Even though the amount of written information is quite abundant, I feel that nothing can really replace the experience of learning by listening to the music. For this reason, I recommend that you listen to the enclosed CD before you start studying the music in this book.

I started playing guitar almost 30 years ago, but I can still clearly remember that sense of jubilance that I felt after learning the first few chords of a new song. I still approach each new piece with a sense of discovery, and feel a sense of accomplishment whenever I complete a new composition. These feelings spark in me a constant joy for playing this wonderful instrument.

I hope that this book will help improve your dexterity, fuel your creativity, and deepen your love for the guitar.

Enjoy,

Peppino D'Agostino

Contents

Contents

Standard Tuning Performance Notes

Calypso-Facto:

I grew up listening to a variety of musical styles, and some of my favorite was the music of Central and South America. The syncopated rhythms, the gorgeous melodies, and the elaborate harmonies are still very fascinating to me. This tune is influenced by these very beautiful and distinctive styles of music. Syncopation is the main characteristic of this composition and before you attempt to play it, I recommend you listen to the included CD in order to absorb the musical pulse and accents.

Note 1: Measure 1

Pay attention to the fact that throughout the song the right hand index, middle and ring fingers are used to play chords on either the 2nd, 3rd and 4th strings or the 3rd, 4th and 5th strings. When you play these chords, the emphasis is usually on the up-beat.

Note 2: Measure 8

Notice that the syncopation is very frequently in the bass line, and is done by alternating the right hand thumb and index finger.

Note 3: Measures 21 - 24

During these measures the left hand ring finger is kept on the 3rd string and is used as a "pivot" finger to build the various positions.

Song for Carol:

I wrote this composition for a very good friend of mine. This is the only guitar duet in this book and I hope that you'll find it enjoyable playing this piece with another guitarist.

Note 1: Measure 3 (First Guitar)

The left hand ring finger is kept on the 5th fret of the 3rd string until the end of measure 8, and it serves as a "pivot" finger for building the various chords.

Note 2: Measure 7 (First Guitar)

The open 1st string at the end of this measure will give you the time to position your left hand fingers so that you can play the large stretch in measure 8.

Note 3: Measure 11 (Second Guitar)

Throughout the tune, the second guitar plays the solo. Sustaining the notes as long as possible gives an evocative and intimate quality to the melody.

Mediterranean Dance:

This composition is a tribute to all the countries touched by this beautiful sea. The music was influenced by the lively rhythms and typical melodies of the solar Mediterranean region, specifically by the "Tarantella" and the "Sardinian Dances."

This tune is particularly difficult to play, because the pace is fast and some of the chords are intricate. Practice the song slowly and pay close attention to the right and left hand fingering.

Note 1: Measure 16

If you don't use a thumb-pick notice that the right hand thumb plays the downstroke in the regular fashion (toward the treble strings), and the upstroke is played with the back of the nail.

Note 2: Measure 24

Starting with the second beat of this measure, I play these bass notes by holding the thumb-pick like a regular flat-pick. If you don't use a thumb-pick, you could play these bass notes by alternating your right hand thumb and index finger.

Note 3: Measure 27

Notice that the right hand middle finger plays the first eighth note of each triplet and the right hand index finger plays the last eighth note of each triplet.

Note 4: Measures 36 - 37

In these two measures, the left hand ring and middle fingers don't move from their position on the fretboard.

Note 5: Measure 65

The second beat of the measure is played with the right hand ring finger which strikes all six strings from bottom to top while holding the full chord. This effect is reminiscent of a cascade of notes created by the harp.

Calypso Facto

Peppino D'Agostino

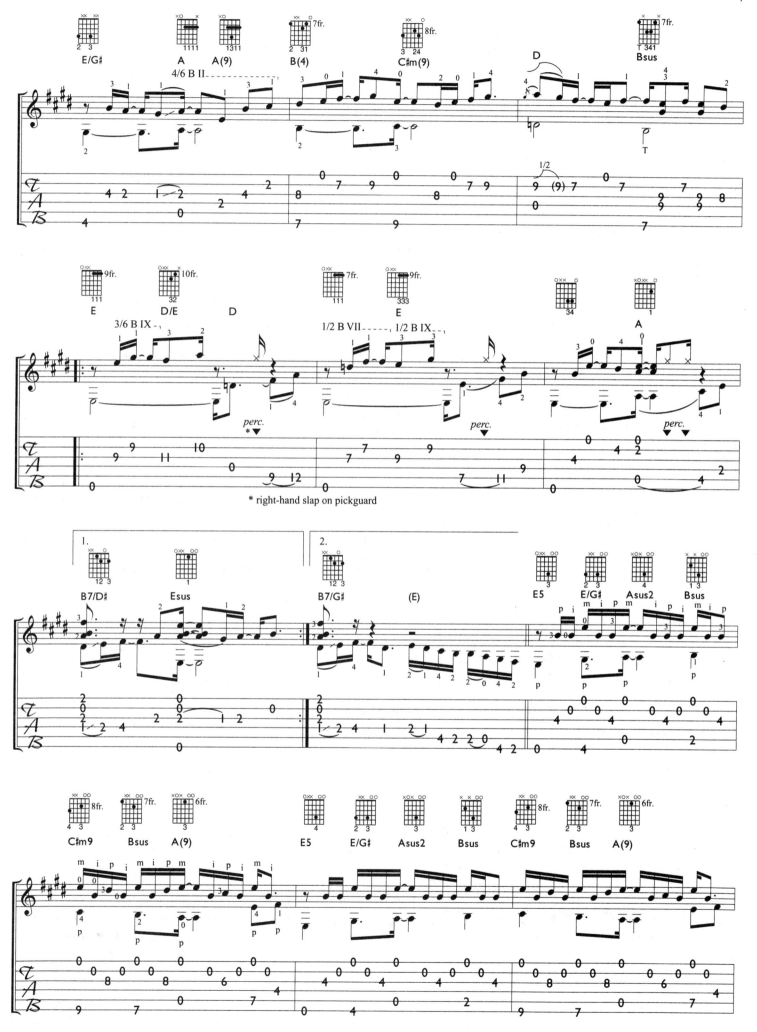

* right-hand slap on pickguard

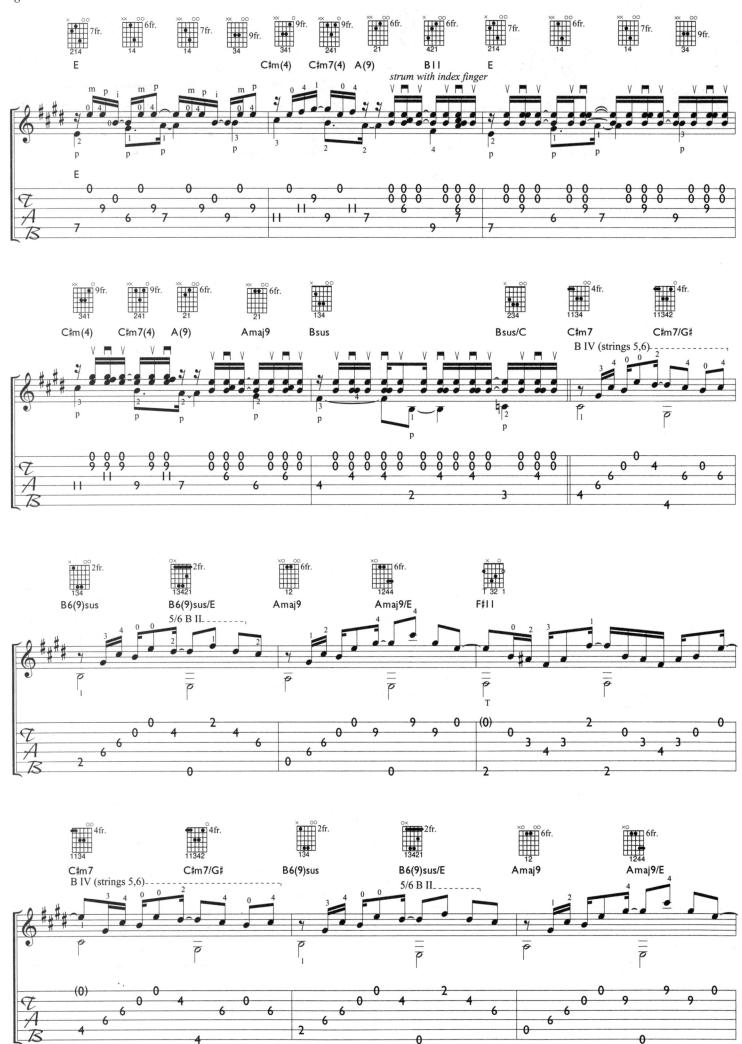

CALYPSO FACTO - 6 - 4

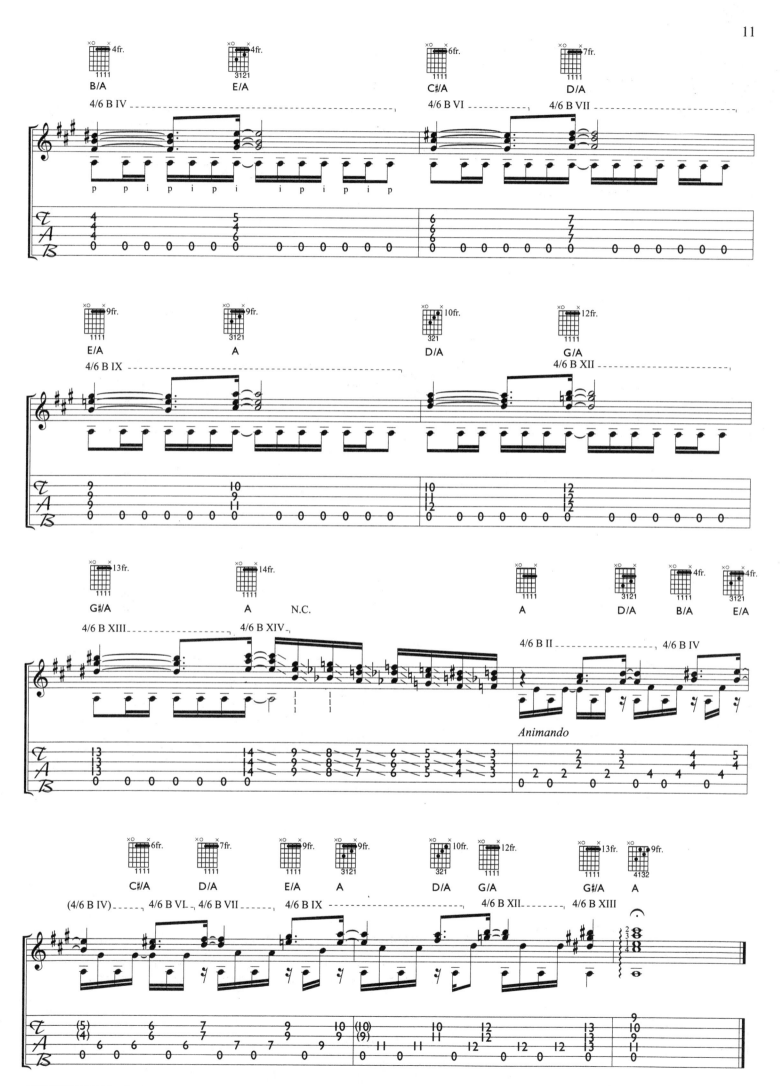

Song For Carol
(Duet)

Peppino D'Agostino

Standard Tuning

Gtr. 2

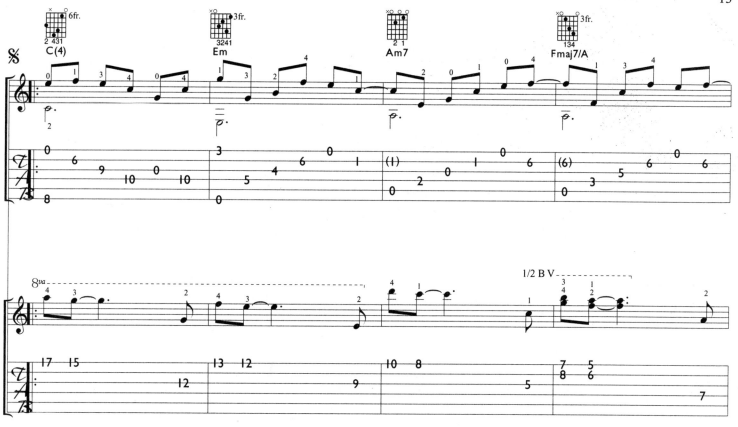

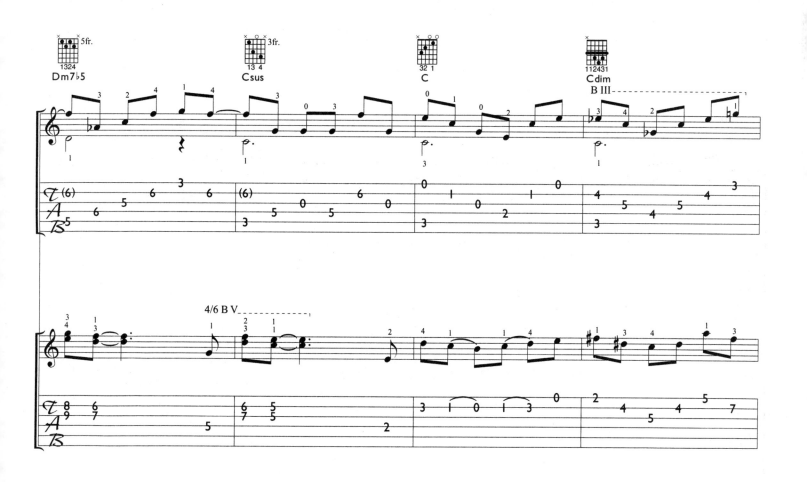

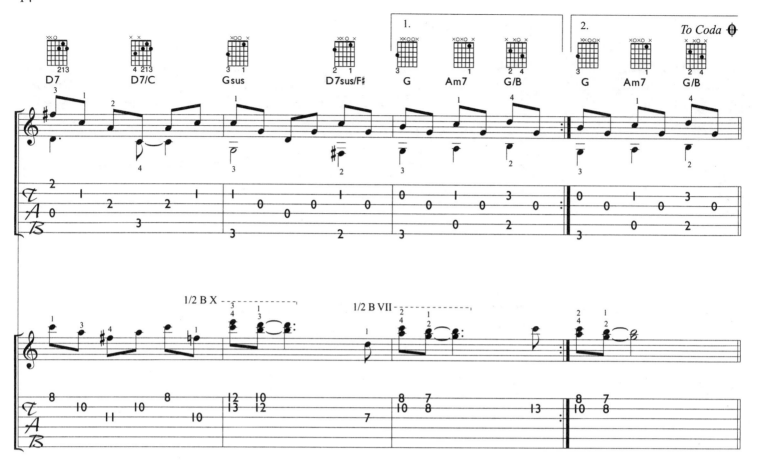

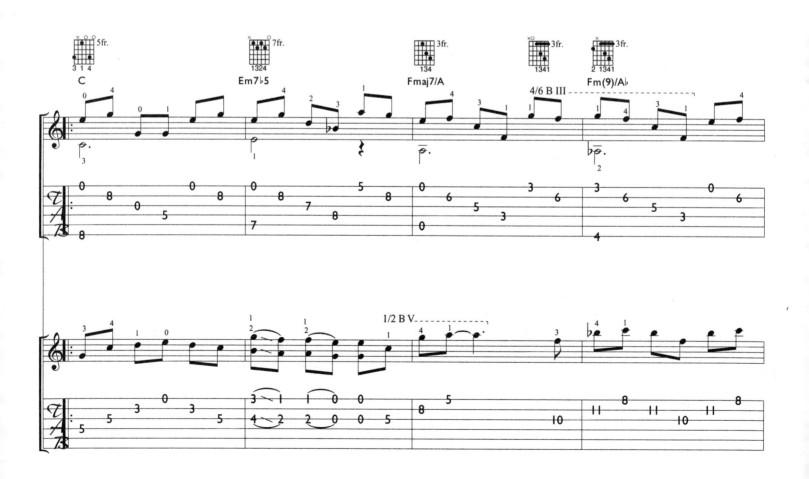

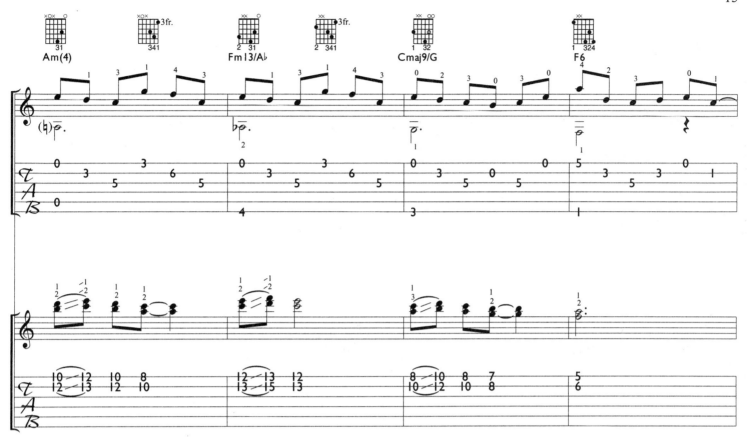

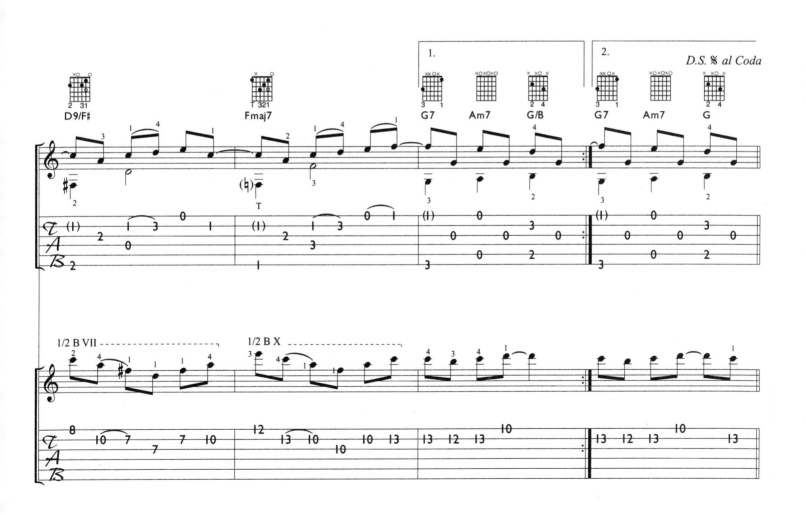

⊕ *Coda*

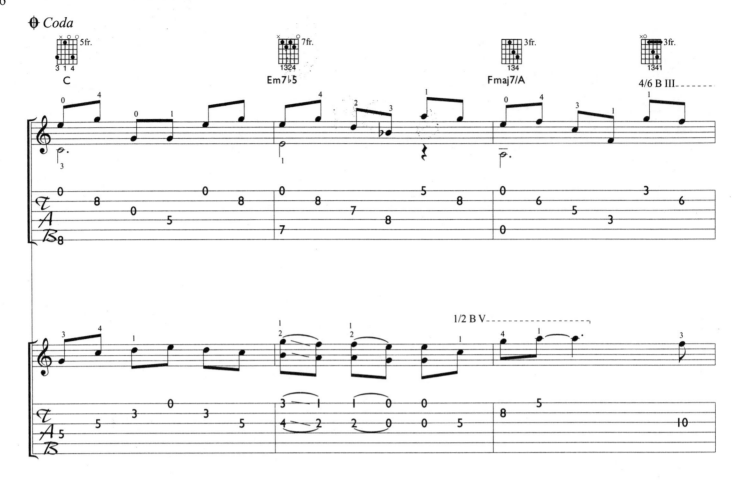

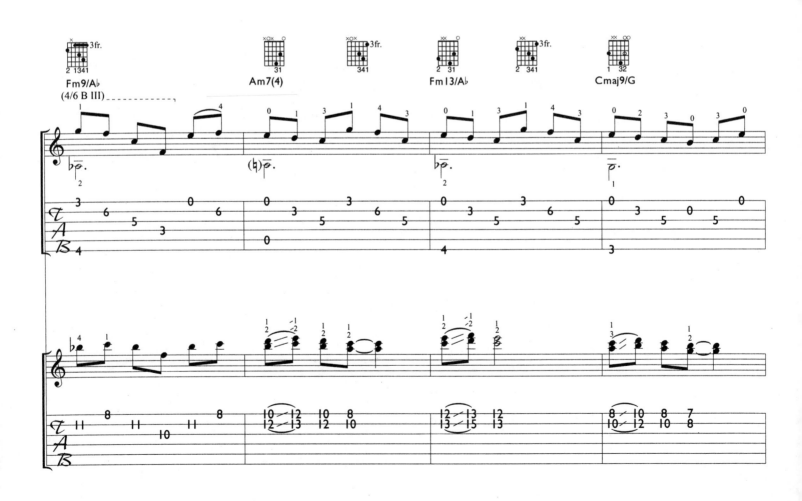

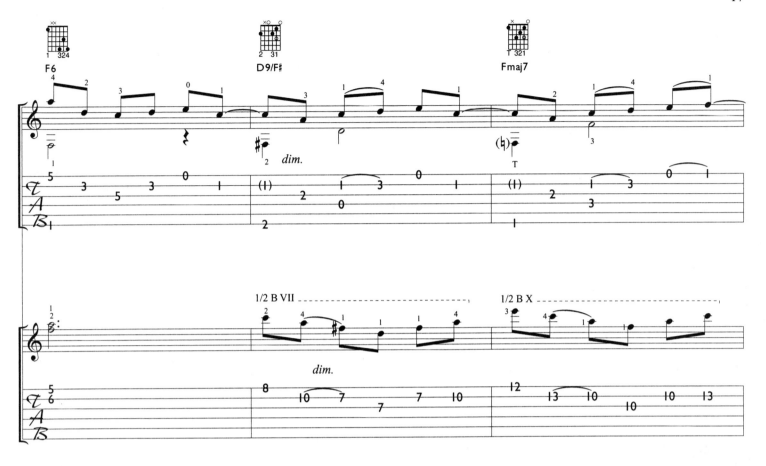

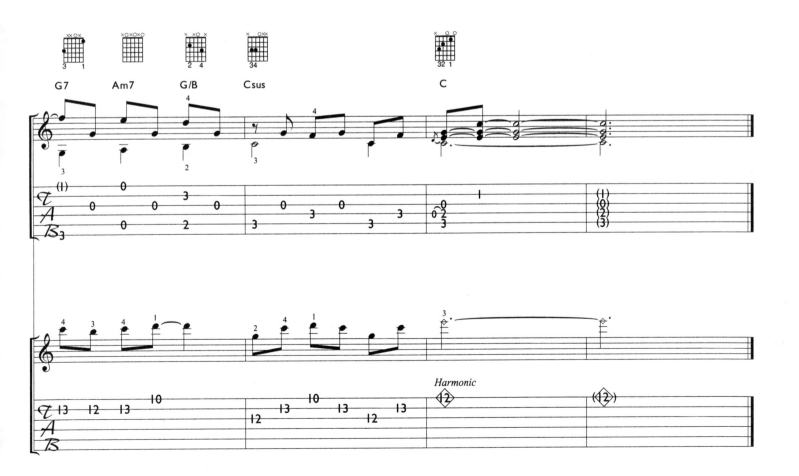

Mediterranean Dance

Peppino D'Agostino

Standard Tuning

MEDITERRANEAN DANCE - 5 - 2

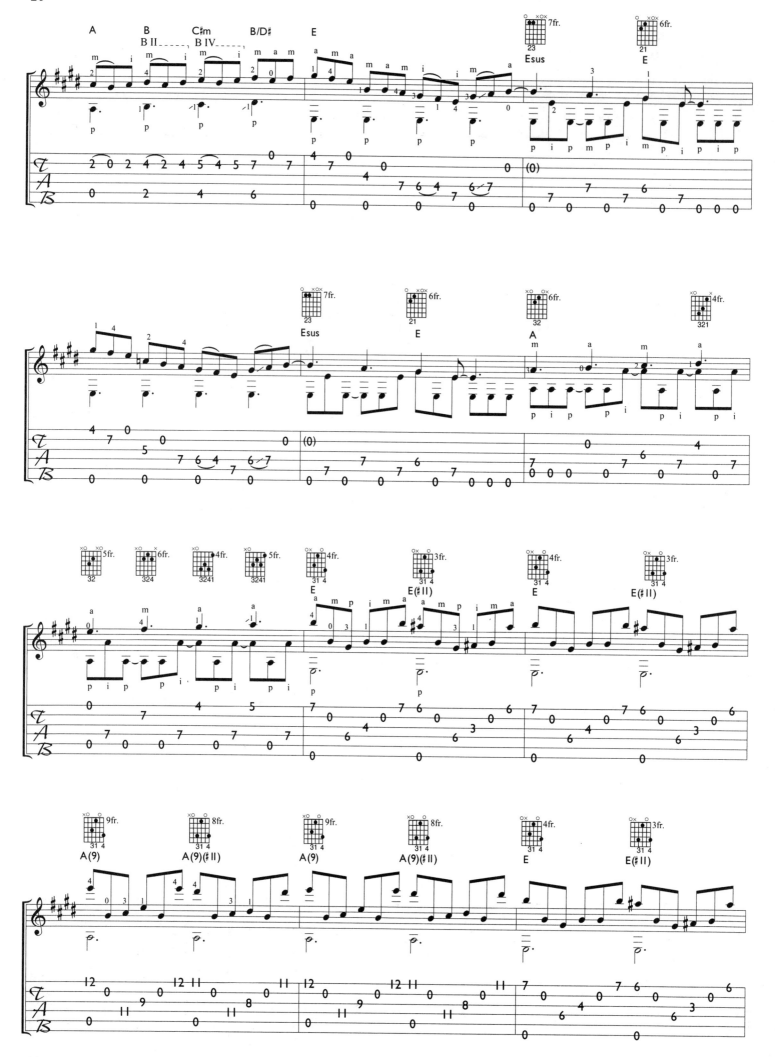

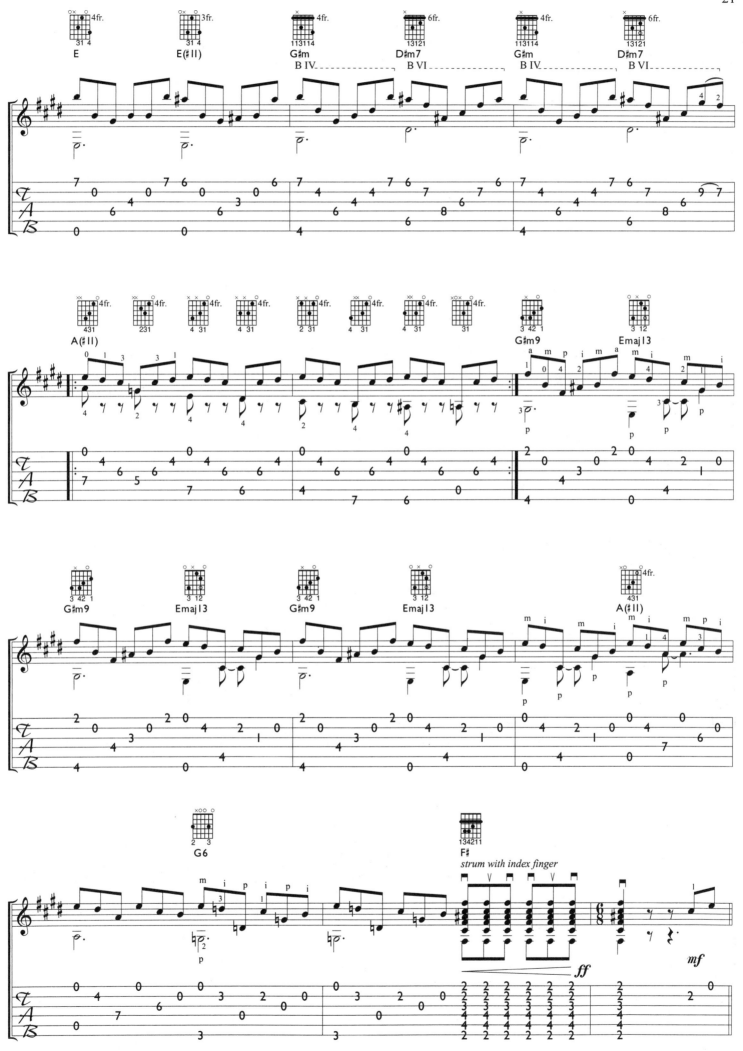

MEDITERRANEAN DANCE - 5 - 4

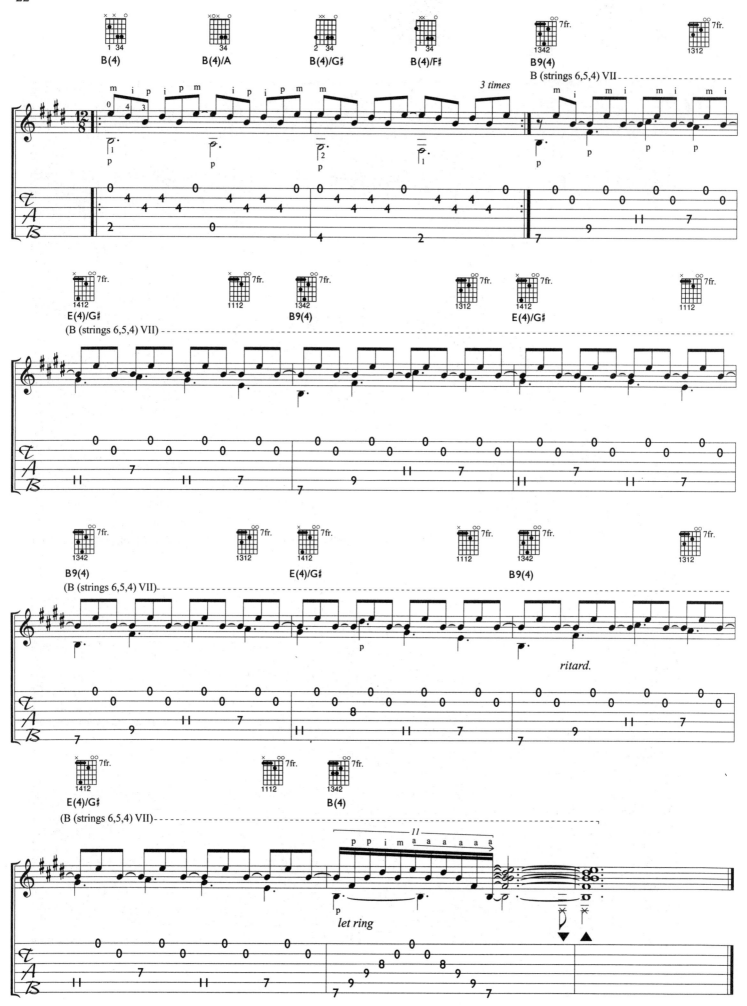

▼ = Slap face of gtr. with index finger.

▲ = Slap side of gtr. with back
of index fingernail.

DADGAD Tuning

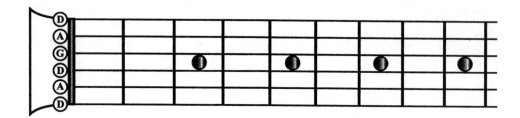

To change your tuning from standard to DADGAD:

- Lower your 6th string a whole step from E to D. The 12th fret on the 6th string (D) should now equal the 4th string open (D).

- Lower your 2nd string a whole step from B to A. The open 2nd string (A) should now equal the 3rd string, 2nd fret (A).

- Lower your 1st string a whole step from E to D. The open 1st string (D) should now equal the 2nd string, 5th fret (D).

Play this simple etude in DADGAD tuning to begin to familiarize yourself with the sound of this tuning.

DADGAD Etude

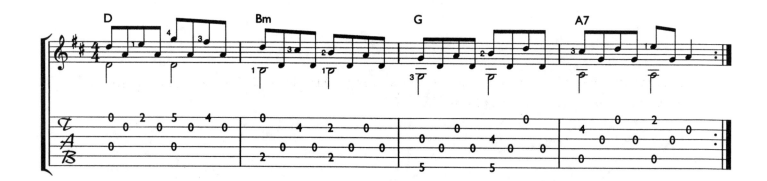

DADGAD Tuning

Here are a few of my favorite chord voicings in DADGAD. Use these voicings to further familiarize yourself with this tuning. Notice the similarities and differences between these voicings and standard tuning. (The 3rd, 4th and 5th strings haven't changed, so notes on these strings remain the same as standard. The 1st, 2nd and 6th strings are down a whole-step so notes on these strings are now located two frets higher than in standard tuning.)

Play through these voicings and see what ideas they stimulate.

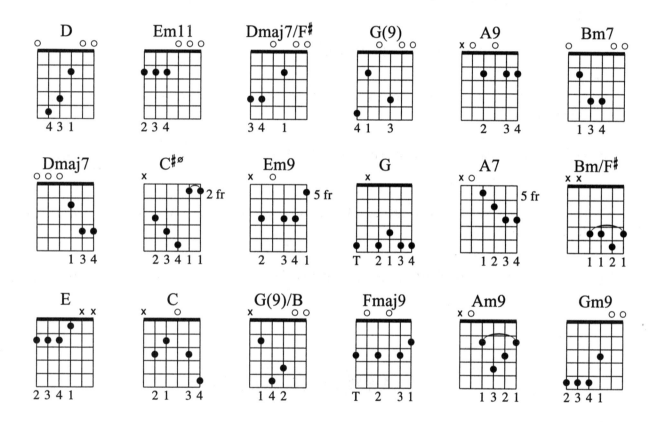

One great way to explore a new tuning is to take a familiar song and work it out in that tuning. Here is my arrangement of Mozart's "Rondo Alla Turka."

Rondo Alla Turka

W.A. Mozart

III Movement
Sonata K. 331

Tuning (Low to high): DADGAD

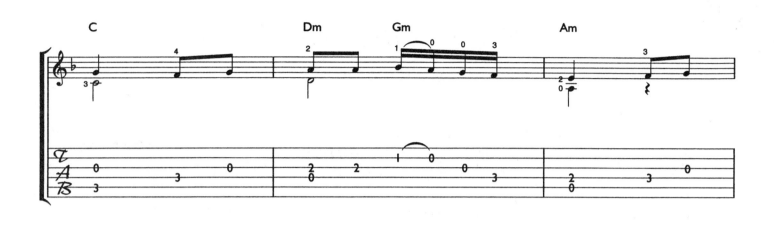

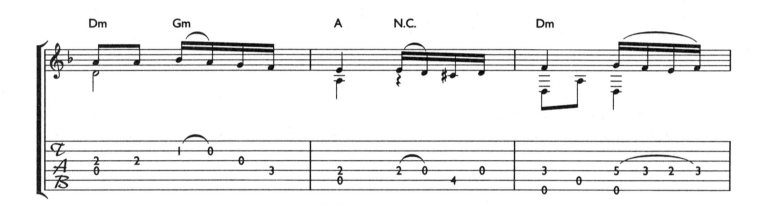

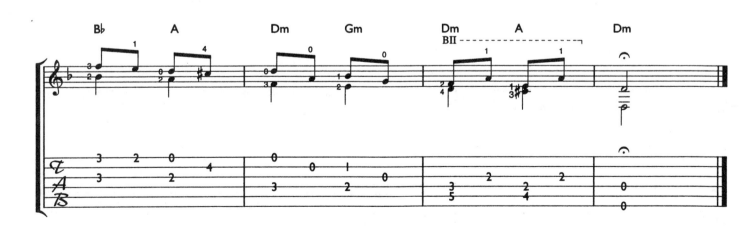

DADGAD Performance Notes

Echo of Delphi Valley

When I was traveling in Greece a few years ago, I had the chance to stop in beautiful Delphi where there is a valley with an amazing natural echo. Inspired by this wonderful setting, I composed this tune in which I use a hammer-on and pull-off technique to try to capture the feeling of that echo. The initial idea that sparked this tune was the bass line which I used as a platform to build the melody. One of the most challenging aspects of this piece is to do the hammers and pulls continuously while changing chords.

Note 1: Measure 1

The descending part of the first beat is played with the right hand ring finger which strikes all six strings from bottom to top until the natural harmonic on the 7th fret of the 6th string.

Note 2: Measure 9

Make sure to play the natural harmonic on the 12th fret of the 2nd string strongly, so that it will ring until the end of the 10th measure.

Note 3: Measure 26

Initially it could be quite challenging to bend the 4th string a 1/2 step (from F♯ to G) with the pinkie. Notice that the 4th string is bent in the direction of the treble strings.

Note 4: Measure 62

The natural harmonic at the 12th fret of the 2nd string is bent by pressing down on the 2nd string with my left hand index finger at the end of the neck between the tuning pegs and the nut. This causes the harmonic tone to rise and fall in an eerie way. Please note that the open 4th string is played at the same time as the bent harmonic is sounded (B), and the open 5th string is played after the left hand index finger has released the bent string, and the harmonic sounds the A note.

Acoustic Spirit

This composition is my way of thanking my guitar and the Great Spirit that comes through her. When I was composing this tune, I tried to create a sound with a texture like rushing wind—a sound that could recall a gentle breeze or the rustling of leaves—to support the melodic line. I found that brushing the strings lightly and continuously accomplished this effect.

Note 1: Measure 2

After playing the harmonics I start "brushing" the first three open strings with the fleshy part of my right hand index finger. This brushing must be very gentle and fluid, like caressing the strings. When the melody starts (played with the left hand only), the "brushing" moves from the first three strings to the 4th, 5th, and 6th strings.

Note 2: Measures 2 & 3

The open 2nd string (note A) and 1st string (note D) are played by pulling the strings with the flesh of the left hand index finger. The other notes on the fretboard are created by hammer-ons and pull-offs.

Note 3: Measure 8

To sustain the notes on the 2nd and 6th string you have to pull-off the open first string which follows with the left hand middle finger.

Note 4: Measure 12

The open 5th string is played with the left hand middle finger to allow the previous note to be sustained.

Note 5: Measure 26

The bass notes are played by "tapping" with the right hand index finger on the 6th string "G" and with the right hand middle finger on the 4th string "G". The position of the right hand fingers looks parallel to the strings.

Note 6: Measure 64

The left hand index finger is used as a "pivot" finger to allow the necessary finger positions for the 9th and 10th measures.

Echo of Delphi Valley

Peppino D'Agostino

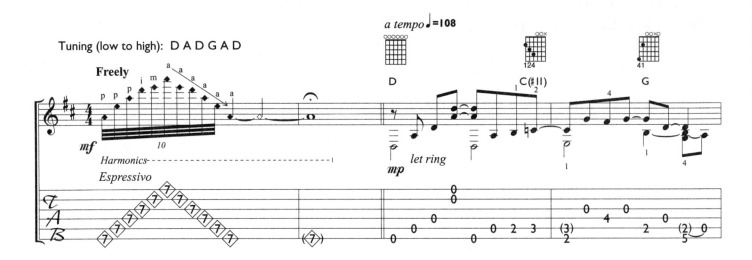

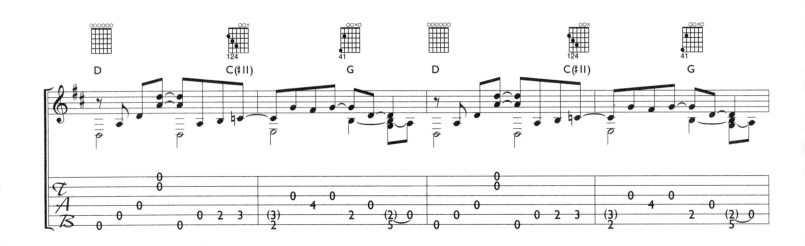

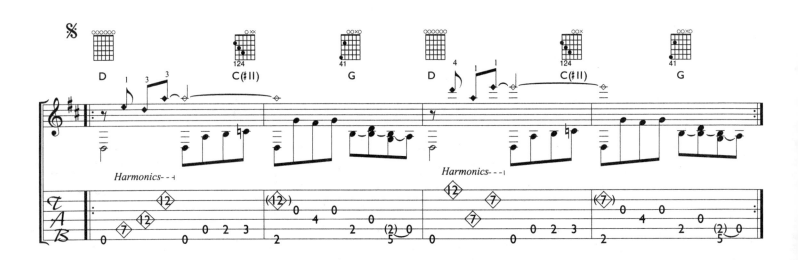

ECHO OF THE DELPHI VALLEY - 6 - 1

ECHO OF THE DELPHI VALLEY - 6 - 2

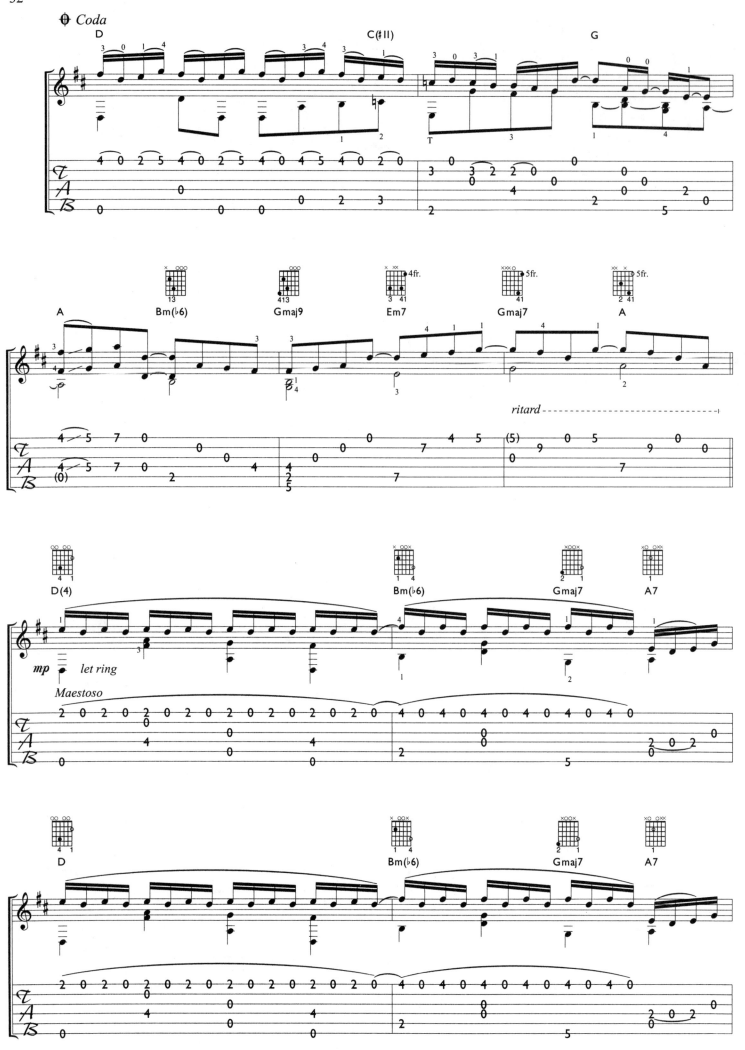

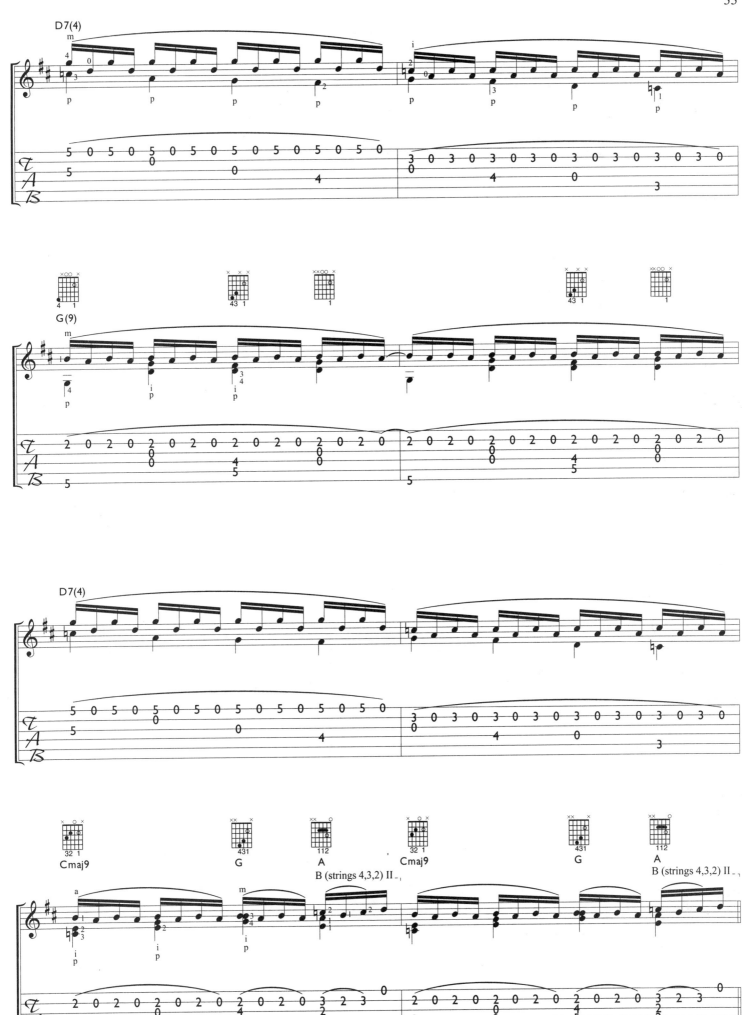

ECHO OF THE DELPHI VALLEY - 6 - 4

34

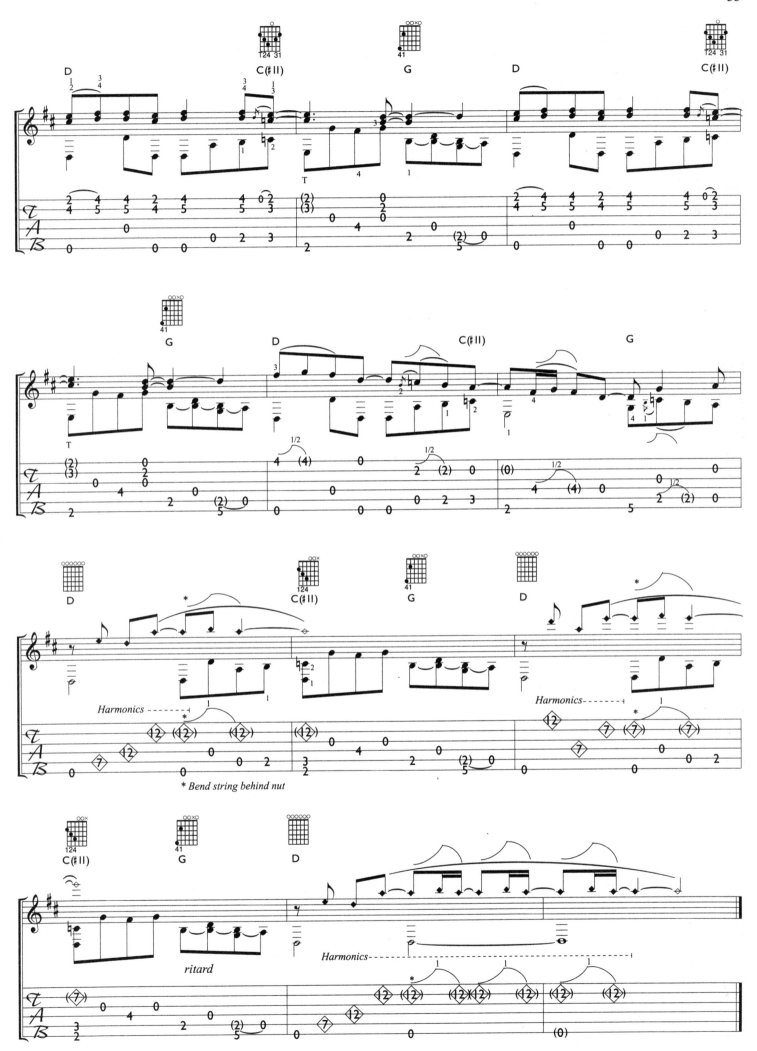

* Bend string behind nut

Harmonics

ritard

Harmonics

Acoustic Spirit

Peppino D'Agostino

Tuning (low to high): D A D G A D

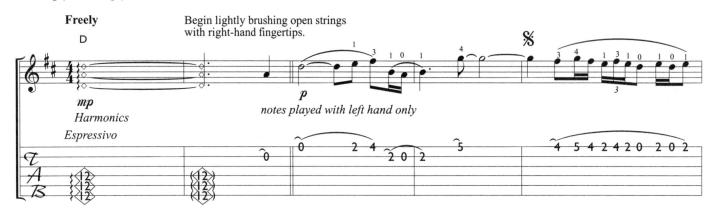

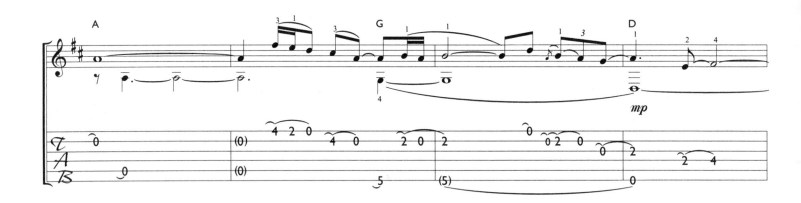

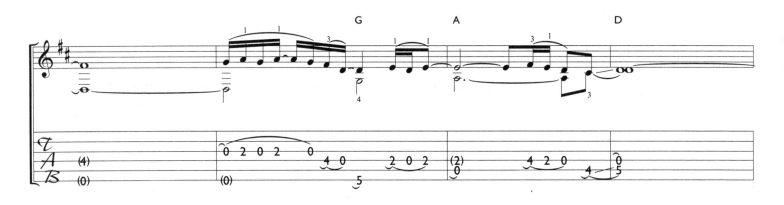

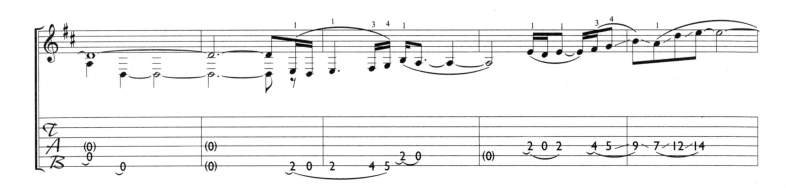

ACOUSTIC SPIRIT - 7 - 1

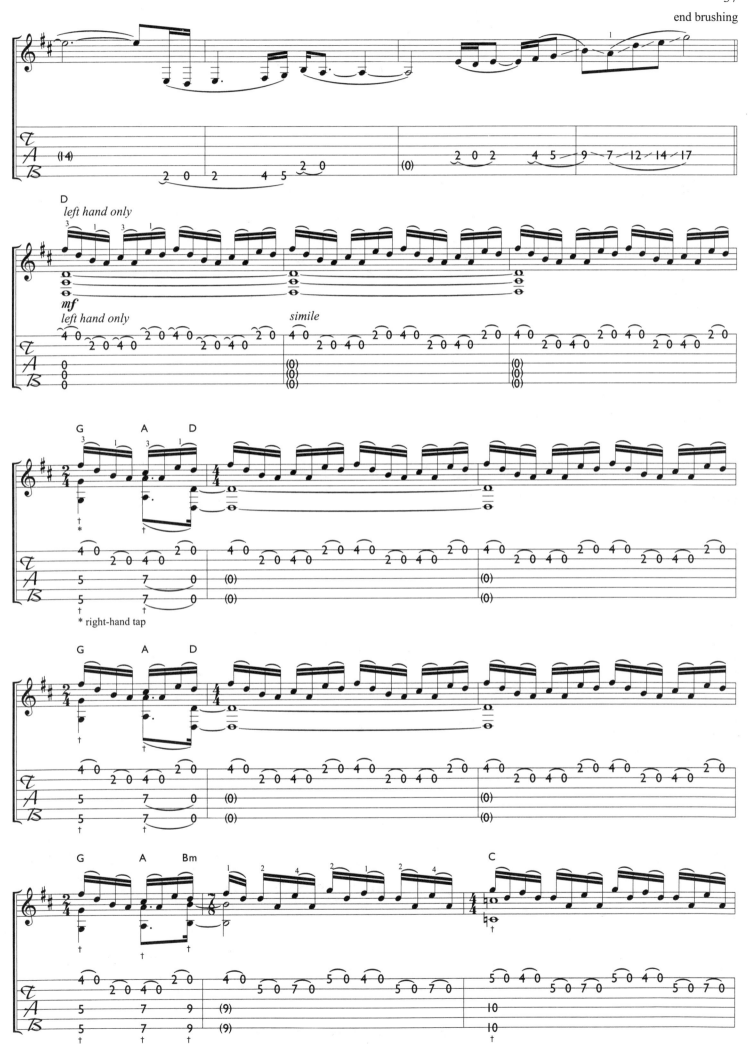

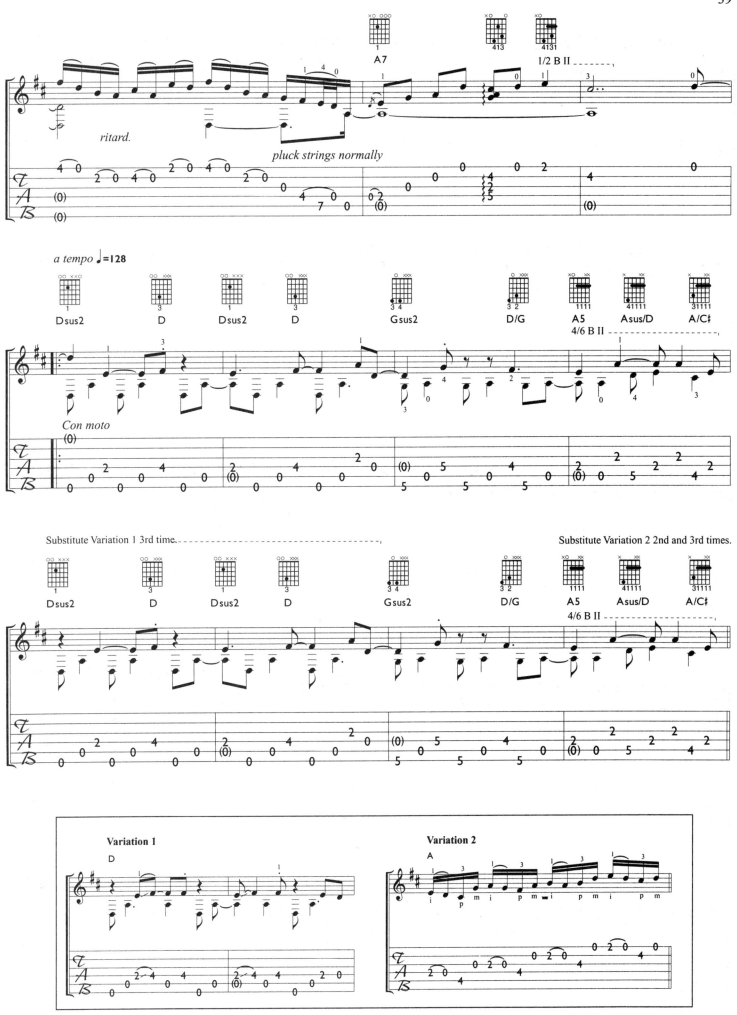

42

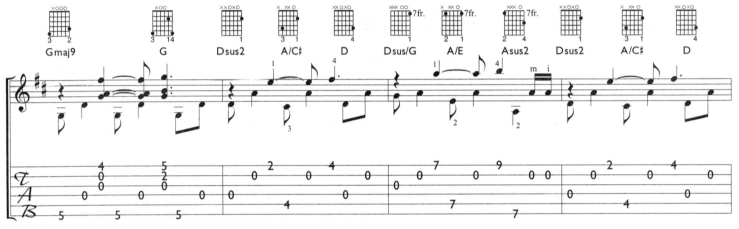

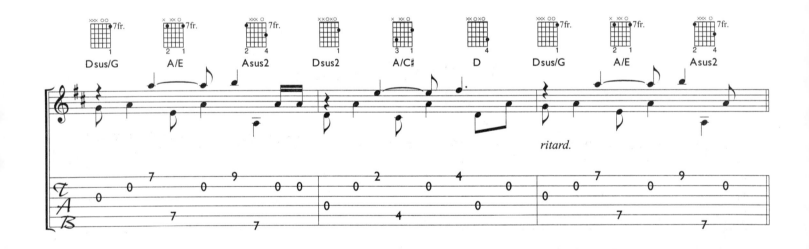

with brushing   *D.S. % al Coda*   **⊕ Coda**

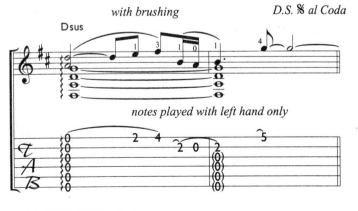

notes played with left hand only

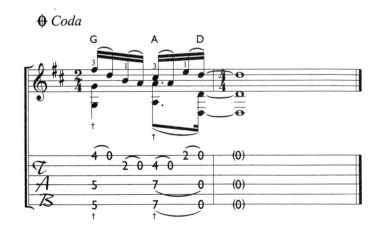

ACOUSTIC SPIRIT - 7 - 7

EBBF#BE Tuning

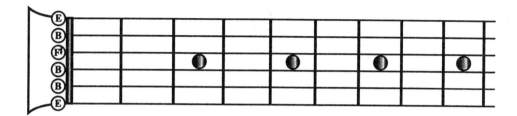

To change your tuning from standard to EBBF#BE:

- Raise your 5th string a whole-step from A to B. The 7th fret on the 6th string (B) should now equal the 5th string open (B).

- Lower your 4th string a step and a half from D to B. The 4th string is now tuned in unison with the 5th string open (B).

- Lower your 3rd string a half-step from G to F#. The open 3rd string (F#) should now equal the 4th string, 7th fret (F#).

Play this simple etude to familiarize yourself with the sound of this tuning.

EBBF#BE Etude

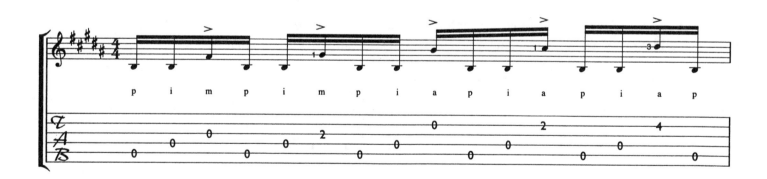

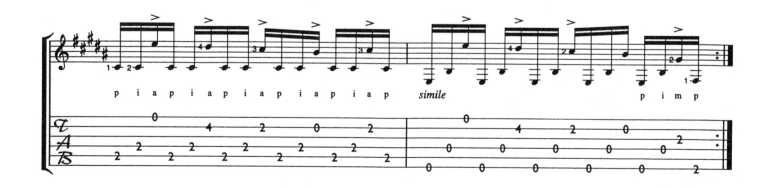

EBBF♯BE Tuning

Here is a nice sampling of chord voicings in EBBF♯BE tuning. Use these voicings to further familiarize yourself with this tuning and see what ideas they stimulate.

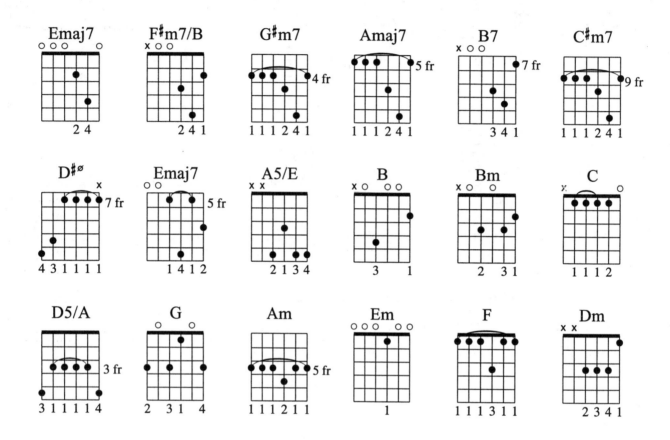

Here is my arrangement of the popular folk standard "House of the Rising Sun." Again, arranging familiar melodies in a new tuning is a good way to acquaint yourself with that tuning.

House of the Rising Sun

Folk Song

Tuning (Low to high): EBBF♯BE

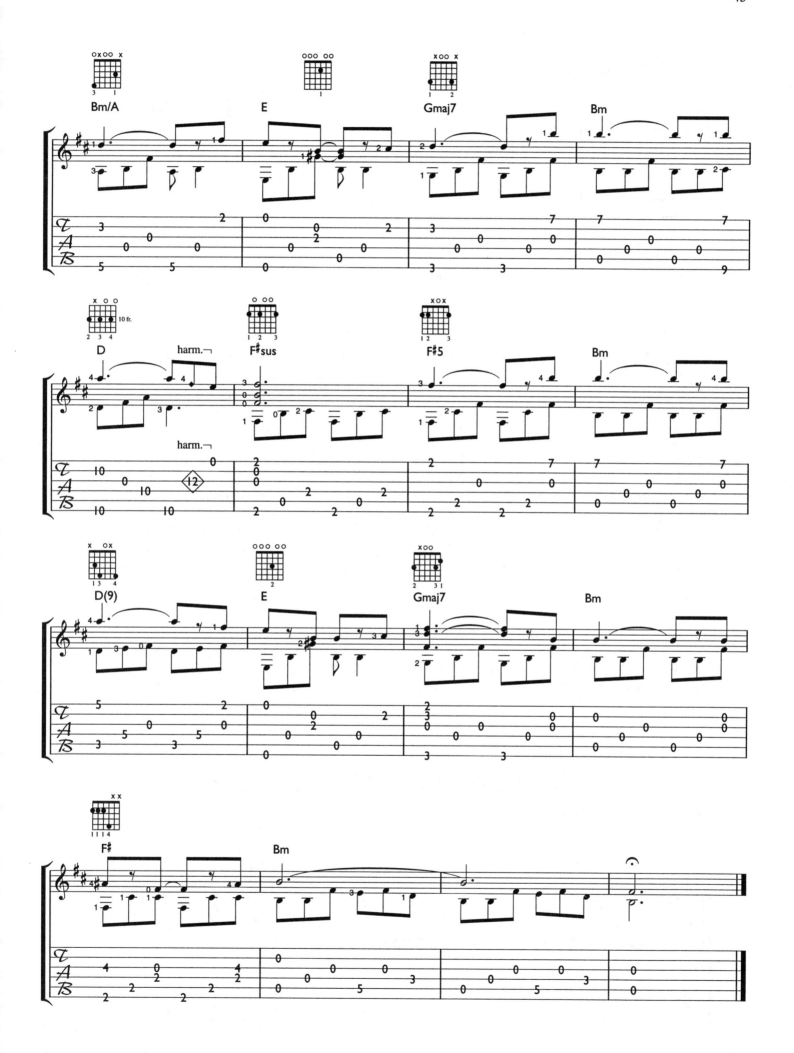

EBBF#BE Performance Notes

Goodbye Robbie:

This composition was written in memory of guitarist Robbie Basho. Sustaining the notes of the melody as long as possible, while maintaining a fluid and constant arpeggio in the bass strings is one of the difficulties of this piece. The notes of the melody are almost always "in levare" (as we say in Italian…meaning in the up beat). This tune will help you to develop a good level of independence between the thumb and the fingers of your picking hand.

Note 1: Measure 4

You should use the right hand thumb to play the 6th, 5th, and 4th string. The index finger plucks the 3rd string, the middle finger plays the 2nd, and the ring finger strikes the 1st. Only when you encounter two subsequent notes on the same string should you play them by using two different right hand fingers.

Note 2: Measures 13 & 14

Starting from the last two eighth notes of measure 13 gradually build the chord fingering by first positioning the left hand index finger (barre position 4/6 on 2nd fret), secondly by placing the left hand pinkie (5th fret of the 5th string) and finally by using your left hand ring finger (4th fret of the 1st string).

Grand Canyon:

This piece is a tribute to a great natural monument. Many years ago Enzo Ponzio, a very good friend of mine in Italy, played one of his compositions for me which had all six strings of his guitar tuned on the note E. I remember being quite impressed by the song. A few years later I wanted to experiment with something similar and I came up with this tuning which has the 5th and 4th string tuned at unison on a B note. This distinctive detail gave me the opportunity to come up with a continuous bass pattern over sustained chords and notes.

Note 1: Measure 5

In the beginning, practice this right hand pattern slowly and with the proper fingering. Speed is definitely an important element of this tune, but accuracy and tone are a lot more meaningful.

Note 2: Measures 23 - 28

These measures are characterized by the so called "asymmetrical" meters typical of the music of the Balkan countries. Pay close attention to the right hand patterns.

Note 3: Measure 35

I play the first two bass notes of the measure by using a rest stroke technique with the right hand thumb. Use a downward movement of your thumb and rest it first on the 5th and then on the 4th string at the conclusion of each stroke.

Peppino D'Agostino

Goodbye Robbie

Peppino D'Agostino

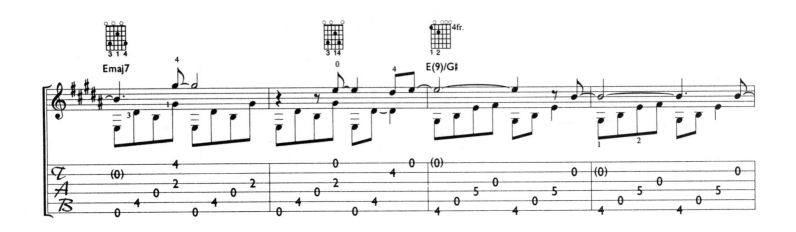

GOODBYE ROBBIE - 4 - 2

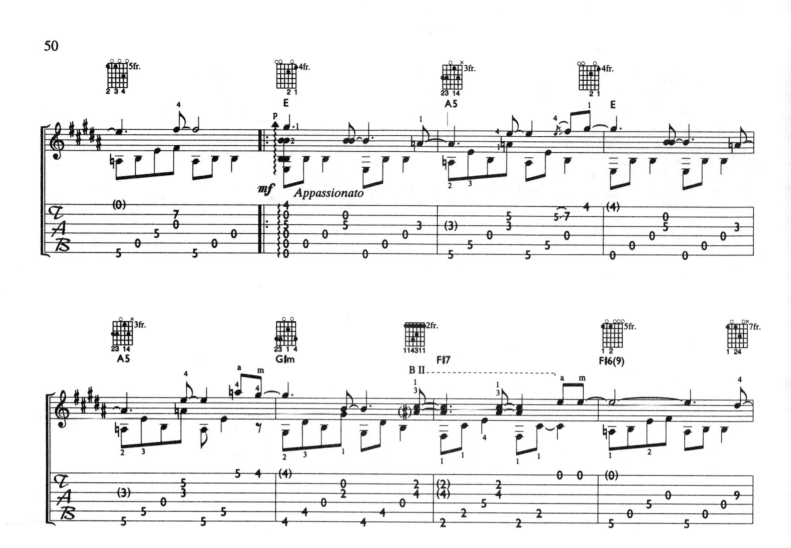

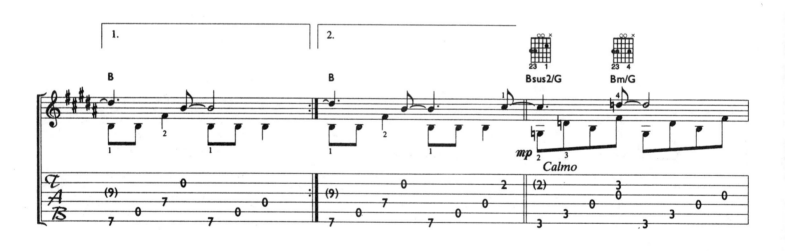

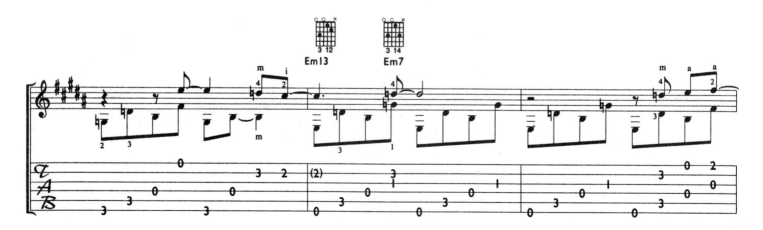

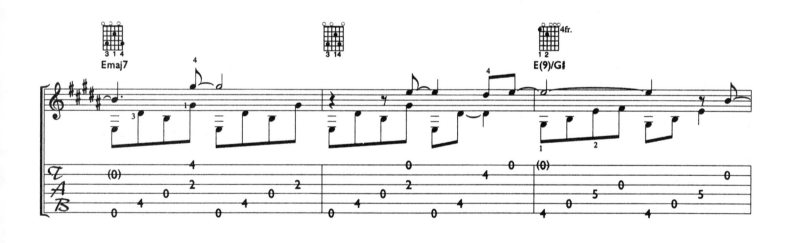

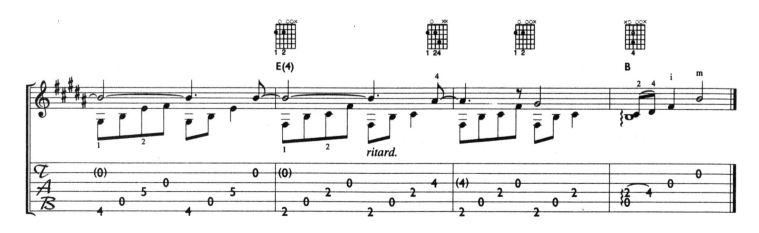

GOODBYE ROBBIE - 4 - 4

Grand Canyon

Peppino D'Agostino

Tuning (low to high): E B B F♯ B E

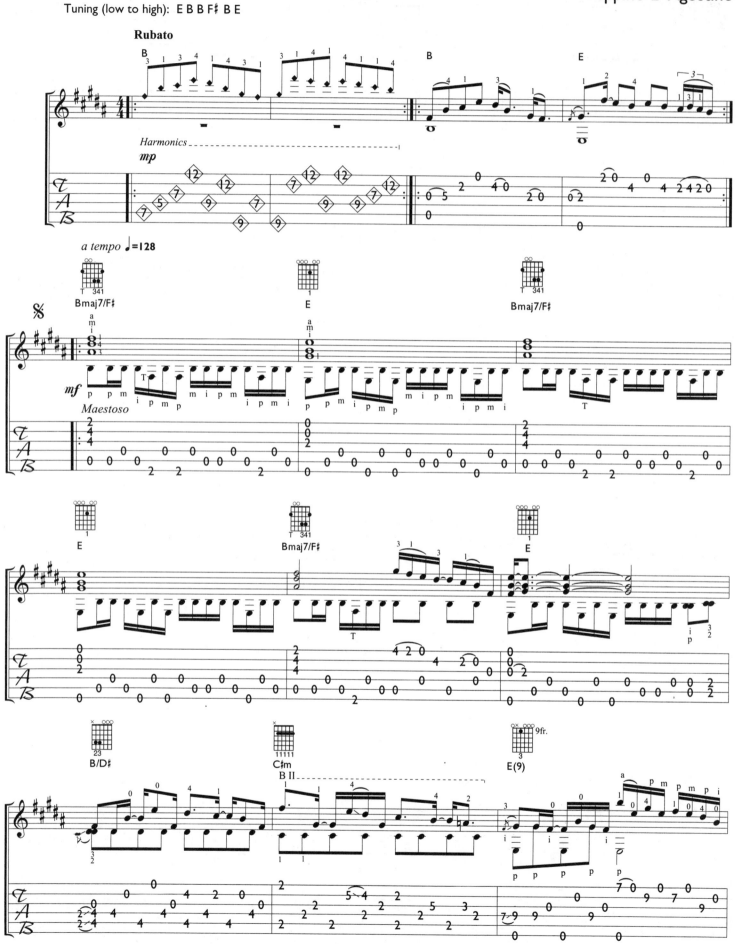

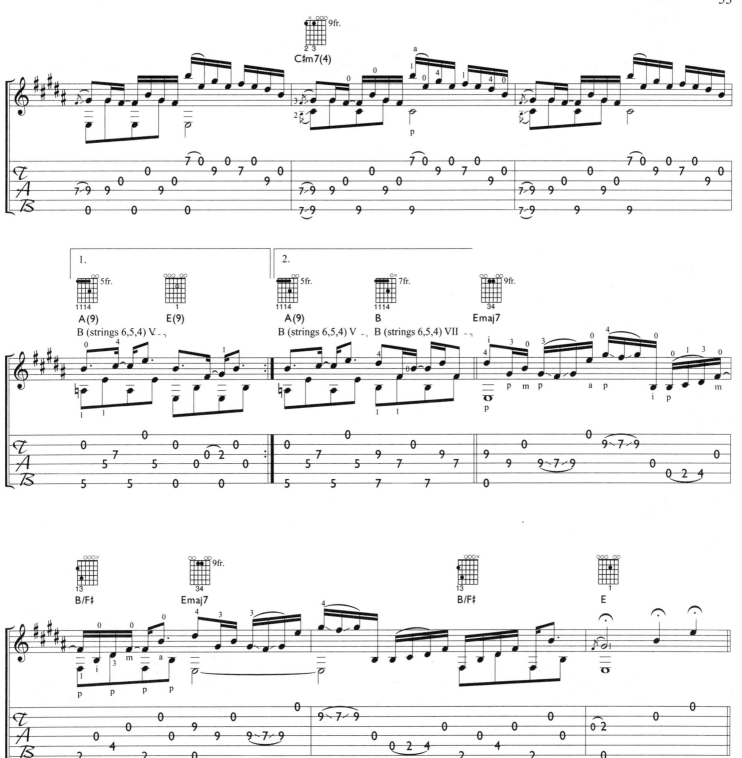

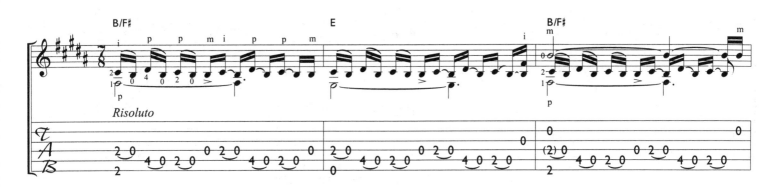

GRAND CANYON - 4 - 2

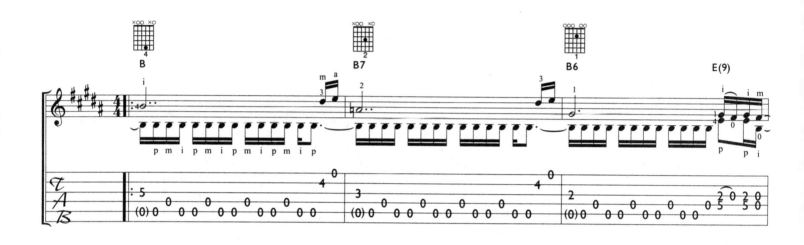

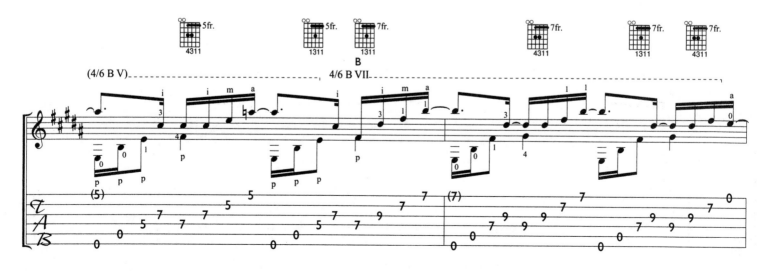

DAC#EBC# Tuning

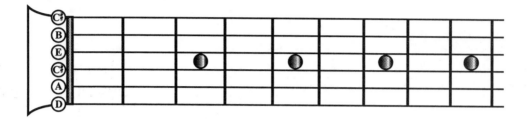

To change your tuning from standard to DAC#EBC#:

- Lower your 6th string a whole-step from E to D.

- Lower your 4th string a half-step from D to C#. The open 4th string (C#) should now equal the 5th string, 4th fret (C#).

- Lower your 3rd string a step and a half from G to E. The open 3rd string (E) should now equal the 4th string, 3rd fret (E).

Play this simple etude to begin to familiarize yourself with the sound of this tuning.

DAC#EBC# Etude

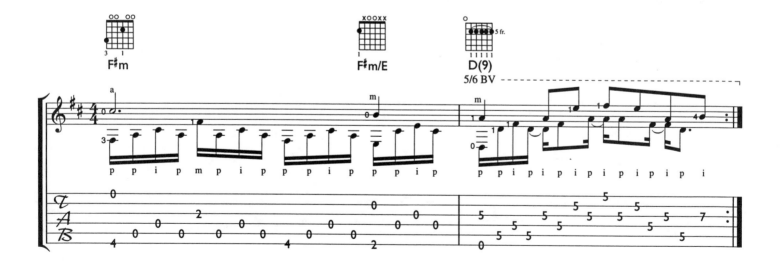

DAC♯EBC♯ Tuning

Here is a nice sampling of chord voicings in DAC♯EBC♯ tuning. Use these voicings to further familiarize youself with this tuning and see what ideas they stimulate.

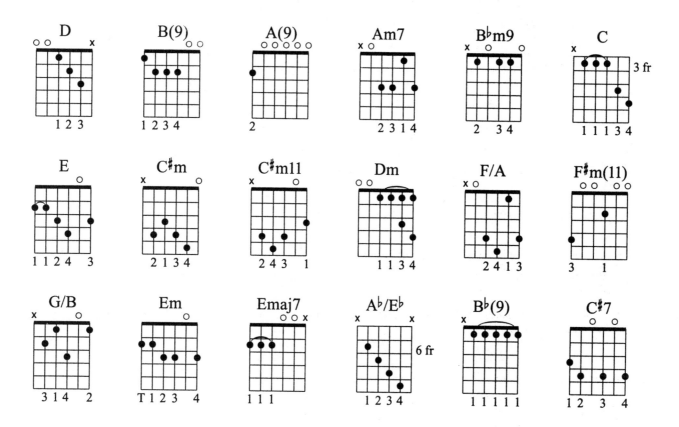

"Silent Night" is a nice example of arranging in this tuning. After learning this arrangement, see if you can begin to expand on it.

Silent Night

Tuning (Low to high): DAC#EBC#

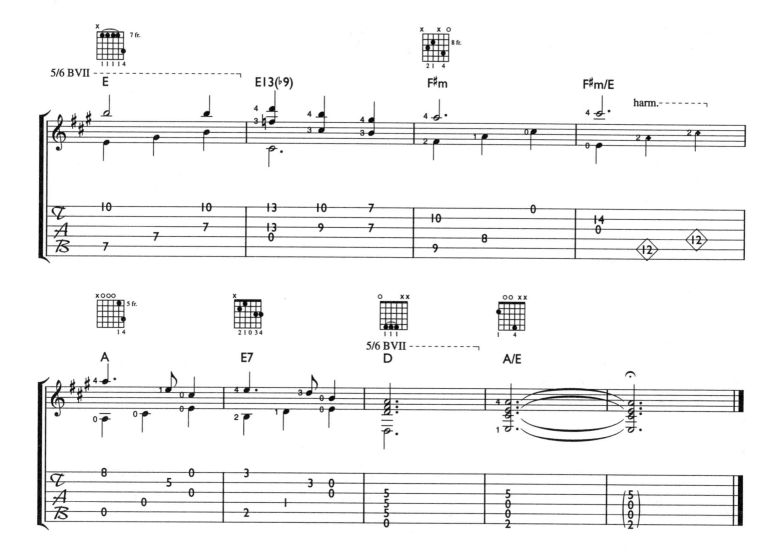

DAC♯EBC♯ Performance Notes

Walk Away Renee:

It was about ten years ago, during a tour on the East Coast, that I first heard this song, performed by my friend singer-songwriter David Wilcox. I immediately loved the melody and the lyrics, but it took ten years until I decided to arrange and record the song with help from David and his wife Nance Pettit.

David sang the song in the key of A and I wanted to come up with an arrangement that was both complimentary to the vocal part and also musically interesting. The tuning that I used for this song really allowed me to feel more creative and inspired, because the resonance of the open strings was striking and the chords were different.

Note 1: Measures 1 - 4

The ascending chromatic bass line on the 4th string needs to be emphasized and sustained. Keep in mind that the fingering I'm suggesting is not the only one. You may find other left and right hand fingerings that work better for you.

Note 2: Measure 46 - 49

The melody played on the 1st string is harmonized in thirds on the 2nd string. The A note, played on the 1st string/8th fret, slides to the 7th fret (G♯), the F♯ on the 7th fret of the 2nd string is simultaneously a pull-off to the 5th fret (E note). This passage is not easy and may require some practice.

After the slide toward the end of the bar, notice that the F♯ (initially played on the 3rd string/second fret using the left hand ring finger) is now played with the left hand middle finger to facilitate the fingering in the next measure.

Walk Away Renee

B. Calilli, T. Samsome and M. Brown

Tuning (low to high): D A C♯ E B C♯

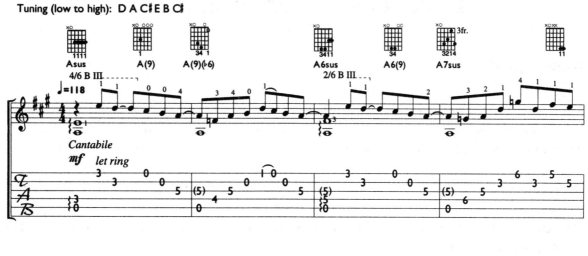

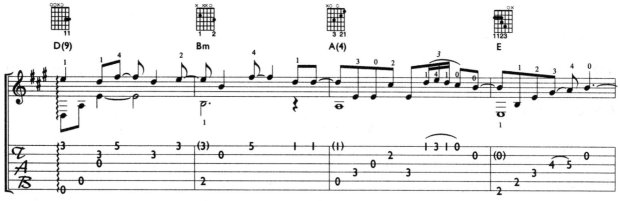

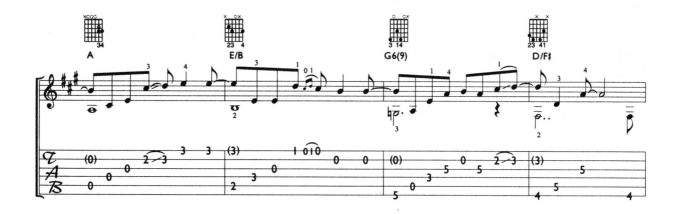

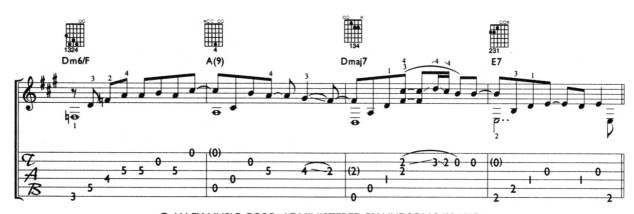

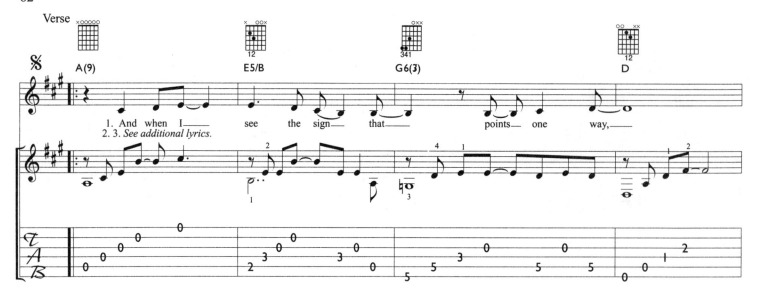

Verse

A(9)　　　E5/B　　　G6(3)　　　D

1. And when I____ see the sign____ that____ points____ one way,____
2. 3. *See additional lyrics.*

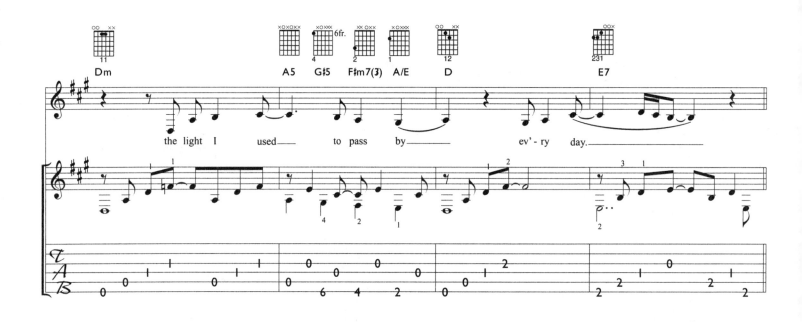

Dm　　　A5　G♯5　F♯m7(3)　A/E　D　　　E7

the light I used____ to pass by_____ ev'-ry day._____

Chorus

A(9)　　　F♯m7　　　D　　　Asus2　　　E5

Just walk a-way____ Re-nee,____ you won't see me fol-low-ing you____ back home.____

63

WALK AWAY RENEE - 5 - 3

Don't walk a - way_____ you won't see me fol - low - ing you_____

Verse 2:

Your name and mine
Inside a heart on a wall
Still find a way to haunt me,
Though they're so small.
(To Chorus:)

Verse 3:

Down deep inside,
The tears are forced to hide.
From deep inside,
The tears are forced to cry.

Last Chorus:

Don't walk away Renee.
You won't see me following you back home.
Now as the rain beats down
upon my weary eyes
for me to cry.

FB♭DFCD (B♭add9) Tuning

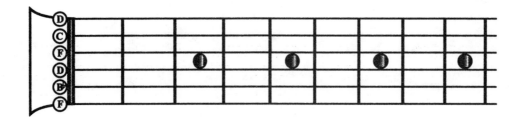

To change your tuning from standard to FB♭DFCD:

- Raise your 6th string up a half-step from E to F.

- Raise your 5th string up a half-step from A to B♭. The open 5th string (B♭) should now equal the 6th string, 5th fret (B♭).

- Lower your 3rd string a whole step from G to F. The open 3rd string (F) should now equal the 4th string, 3rd fret (F).

- Raise your 2nd string up a half-step from B to C. The open 2nd string (C) should now equal the 3rd string, 7th fret (C).

- Lower your 1st string a whole-step from E to D. The open 1st string (D) should now equal the 2nd string, 2nd fret (D).

This is a particularly pretty tuning. The open strings form a B♭add9 chord. Play this etude to begin to familiarize yourself with the sound of this tuning.

FB♭DFCD (B♭add9) Etude

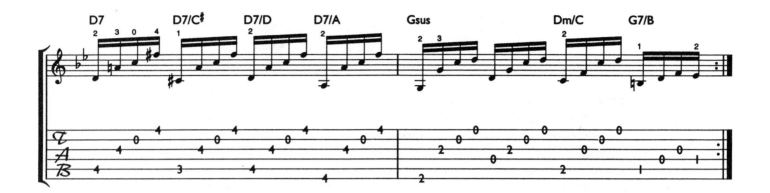

FB♭DFCD Tuning

Here are a few of my favorite chord voicings in FB♭DFCD. Use these voicings to further familiarize youself with this tuning and see what ideas they stimulate.

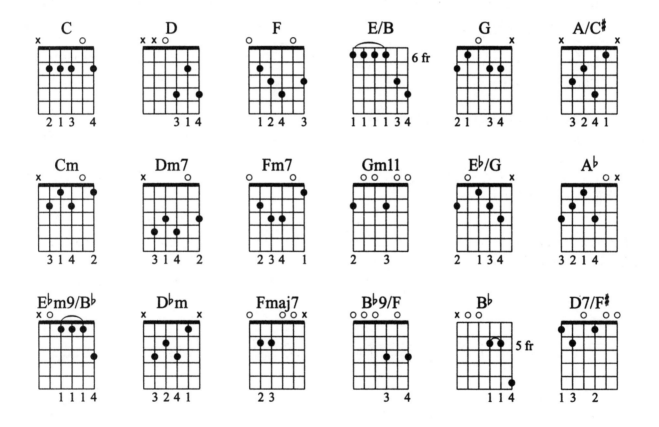

Here is my arrangement of "Mademoiselles De Paris." This is a waltz in B♭ and makes for a simple, but effective use of this tuning.

68

Mademoiselles de Paris

Tuning (Low to high): FB♭DFDC

FB♭DFCD (B♭add9) Performance Notes

Aleza's Eyes:

This tune was inspired by the beautiful eyes of my daughter…

Note 1: Measures 23 & 24

These two measures are played with a technique that is reminiscent of Flamenco guitar style. While holding the chord, play the first bass note (F) with the right hand index finger and use the back of the nail in a downward stroke toward the treble strings. This first movement is followed by playing the 4th, 5th and 6th strings with the flesh of the right hand middle finger in an upward stroke towards the bass notes. The third movement is performed with the flesh of the right hand index finger playing the 5th and 6th string in an upward stroke towards the bass notes. This roll is repeated until the end of measure 8.

Note 2: Measures 25 - 33

The melody here is played on the 4th, 5th and 6th strings, while the arpeggio played on the treble strings creates a framework on which the melody lays.

Close to Heaven:

One of the most difficult things for me is to come up with are titles. When my friend Alfredo Morabito composed the first part of this tune he called it B for lack of ideas! A few years later, I added the second part. I felt that the title needed to be changed. One day I was visiting Torino, Italy, and while I was walking, I saw a huge publicity billboard on the side of the street. The sign said "Il Paradiso e' sulla Terra": which means "Heaven is on Earth," this was the inspiration for the "Close to Heaven." This is a slow tune, and you should let the notes resonate as long as possible so you can create an overlapping layer of sounds.

Note 1: Measure 16

The bass note (G) is played with the left hand thumb. The B is played on the first string, 8th fret with the left hand pinkie. This is a big stretch!

Note 2: Measures 22 - 29

The artificial harmonics and bass notes in these measures are played in the following manner. The left hand fingers the chord forms. The right hand performs three distinctive techniques: 1. The index finger lightly touches (without pressing) the 1st and 2nd string on the 13th and 14th fret. 2. The ring finger plucks the note "determined" by the index finger. 3. The thumb plays the bass strings.

Aleza's Eyes

Peppino D'Agostino

Tuning (low to high): F Bb D F C D

ALEZA'S EYES - 6 - 2

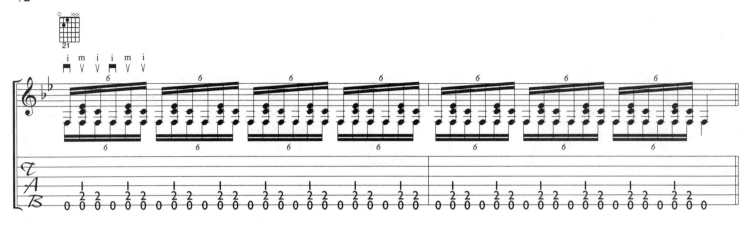

a tempo ♩=94

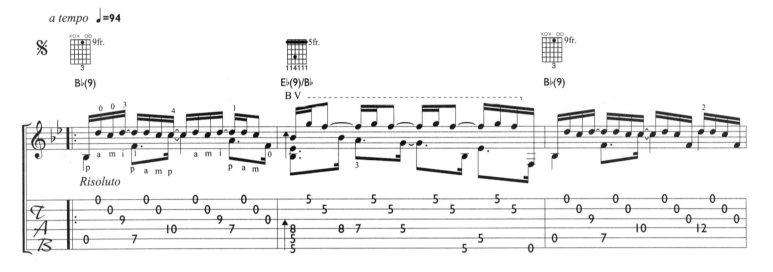

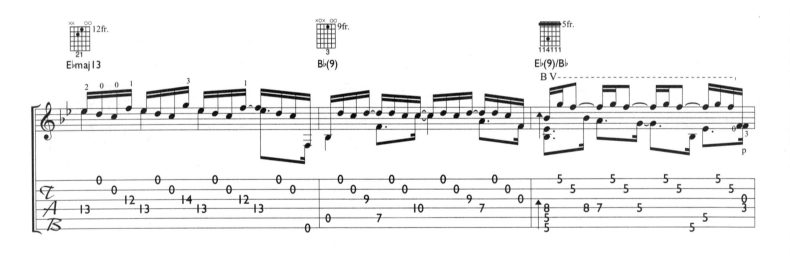

74

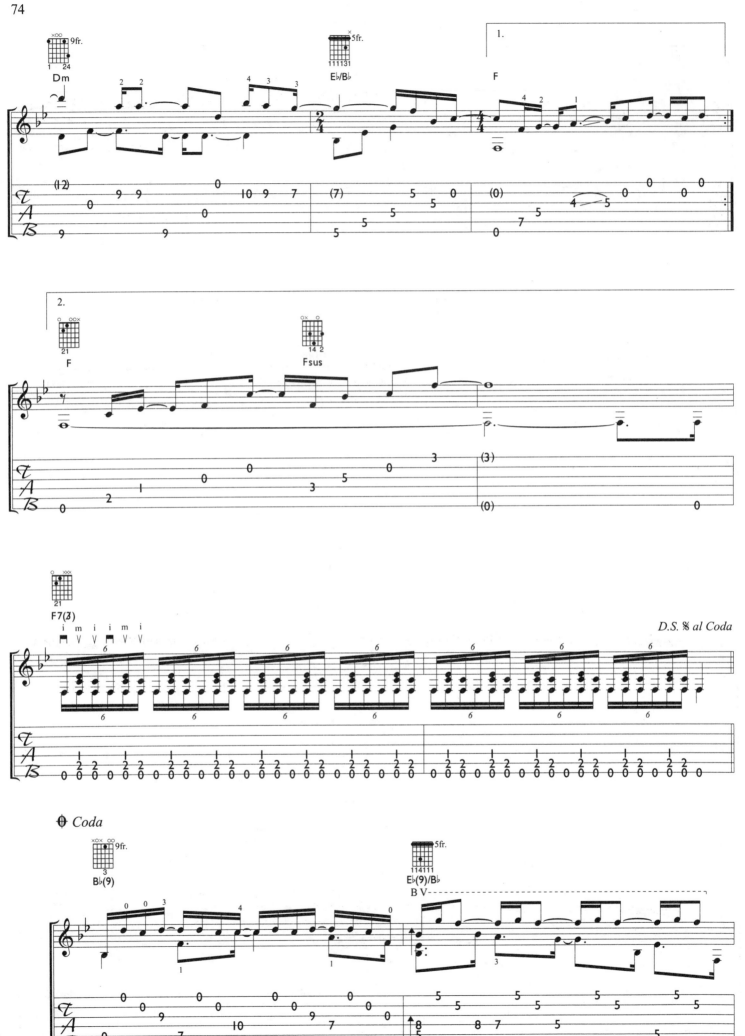

ALEZA'S EYES - 6 - 5

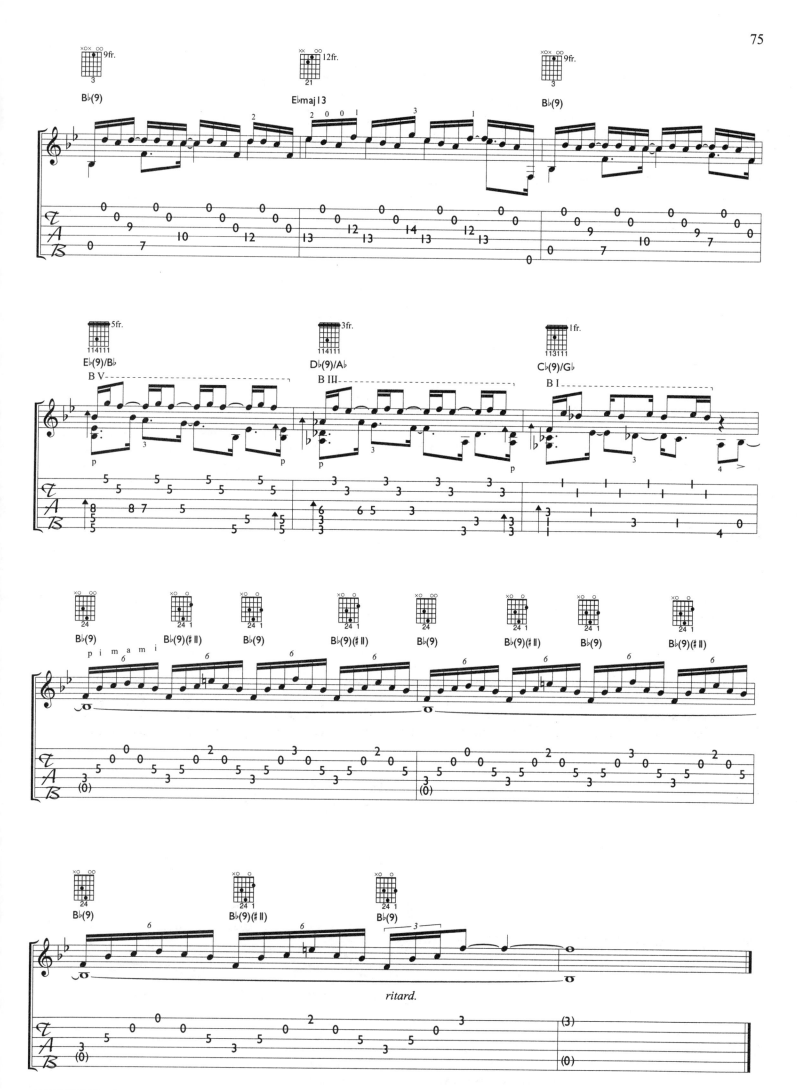

Close To Heaven

Peppino D'Agostino/Alfredo Morabito

Tuning (low to high): F B♭ D F C D

* Thumb in front of neck.

* Fretted notes shown in parentheses.

78

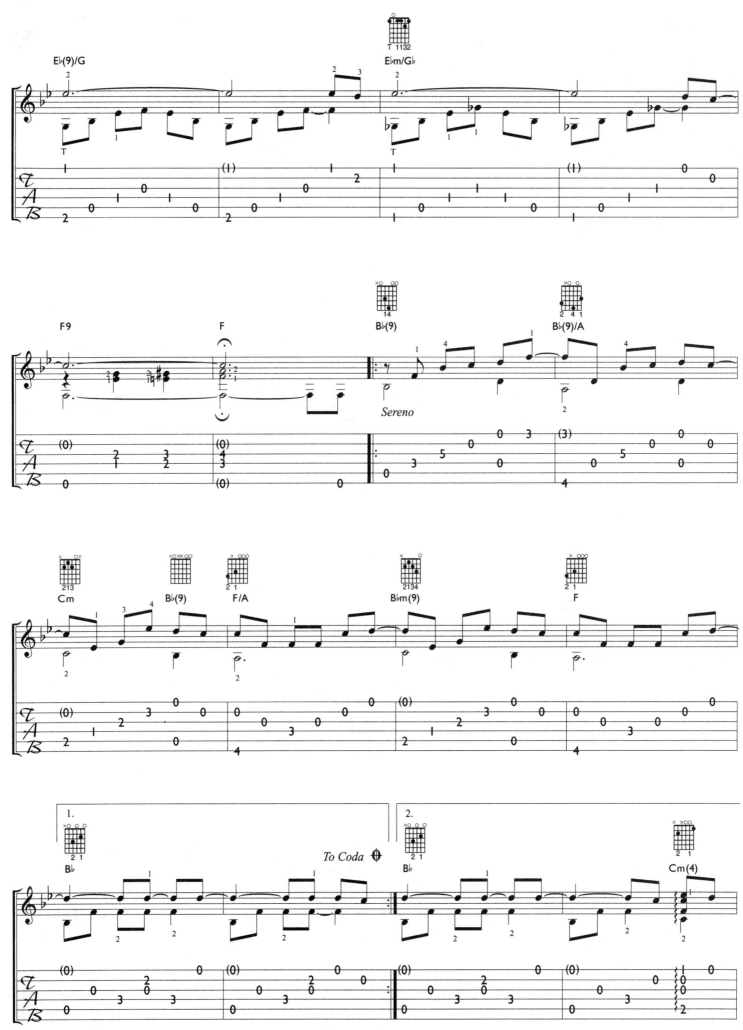

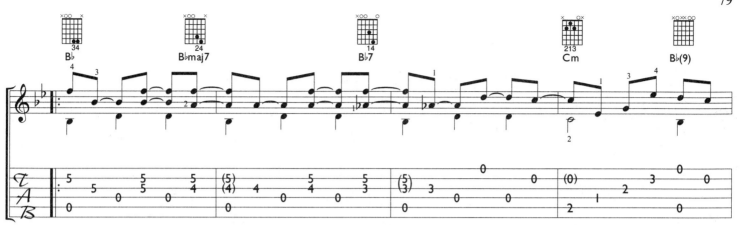

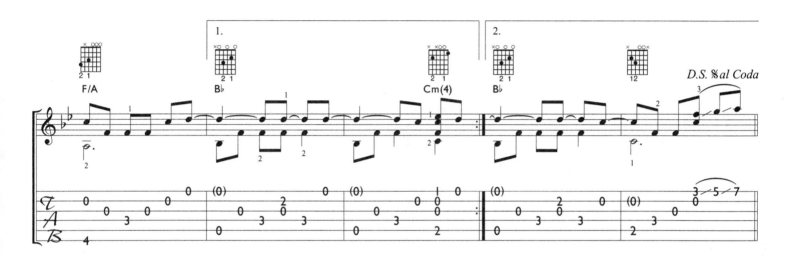

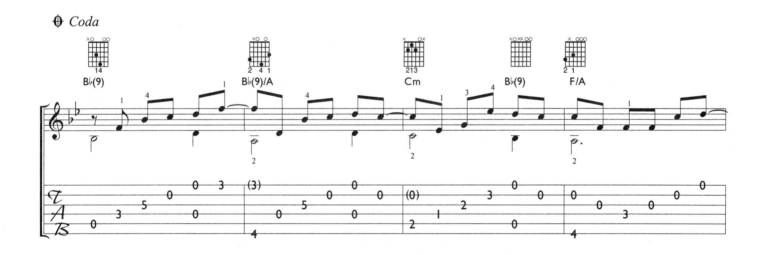

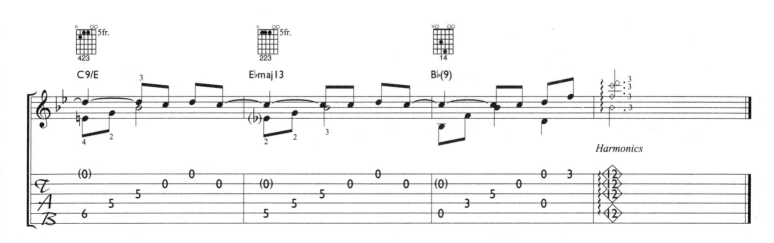

CLOSE TO HEAVEN - 4 - 4

DADF#AD ("D") Tuning

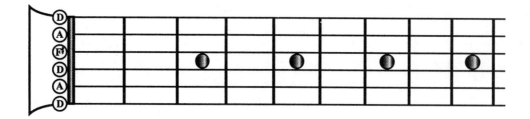

To change your tuning from standard to DADF#AD (also known as "D" tuning):

- Lower your 6th string a whole-step from E to D. The 12th fret on the 6th string (D) should now equal the 4th string open (D).

- Lower your 3rd string a half-step from G to F#. The 4th fret on the 4th string (F#) should now equal the open 3rd string (F#).

- Lower your 2nd string a whole-step from B to A. The open 2nd string (A) should now equal the 3rd string, 3rd fret (A).

- Lower your 1st string a whole-step from E to D. The open 1st string (D) should now equal the 2nd string, 5th fret (D).

This is one of the most common altered tunings. The open strings form a D major chord so a straight barre across all six strings at any fret forms a major chord. Play this etude in "D major" to begin to familiarize yourself with the sound of this tuning.

DADF#AD ("D") Etude

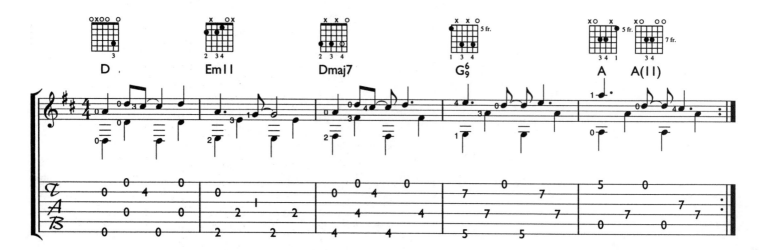

DADF♯AD Tuning

Here are a few of my favorite chord voicings in DADF♯AD. Use these voicings to further familiarize youself with this tuning.

Again, play through these voicings and see what ideas they stimulate.

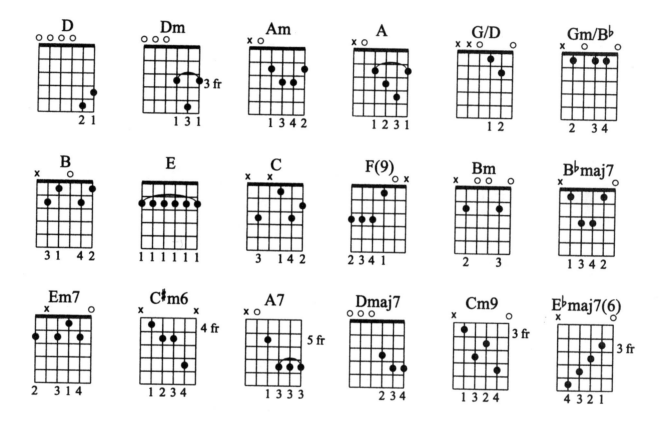

One great way to explore a new tuning is to take a familiar song and work it out in that tuning. Here is my arrangement of Scott Joplin's "The Entertainer."

The Entertainer

Scott Joplin

Tuning (Low to high): DADF♯AD

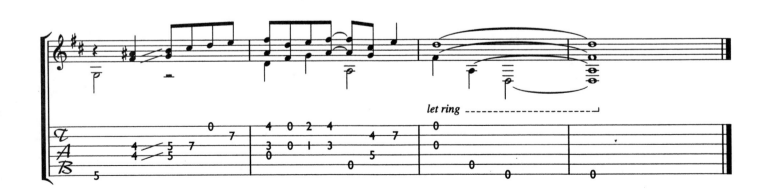

DADF♯AD ("D") Performance Notes

Bella Donna:

This composition was written for Donna for all her help and support… This tune is very lively and quick. To achieve the speed and the dynamics, a careful attention to both the right and left hands is required. We were very careful in indicating the appropriate fingerings to use, considering the fact that among other technical difficulties, the index or middle finger often substitutes the thumb in the bass line (which can be a little disorienting for some players).

Note 1: Measure 7

In this measure you have an example of right hand string stopping technique which I use extensively during this piece. After playing the first eighth note of the second beat (4th string open) with your right hand middle finger, you have to stop the same string with the flesh of the right hand index, and then play the last eighth note of the triplet (4th string open), with the nail of your right hand index finger.

Note 2: Measures 46 & 47

The notes that slide on the 4th string are not very easy to execute considering the distance between them (sometimes 12 frets). A fraction of a second before the performance of these passages, look at the "destination fret" to facilitate the slide.

Bella Donna

Peppino D'Agostino

Tuning (low to high): D A D F# A D

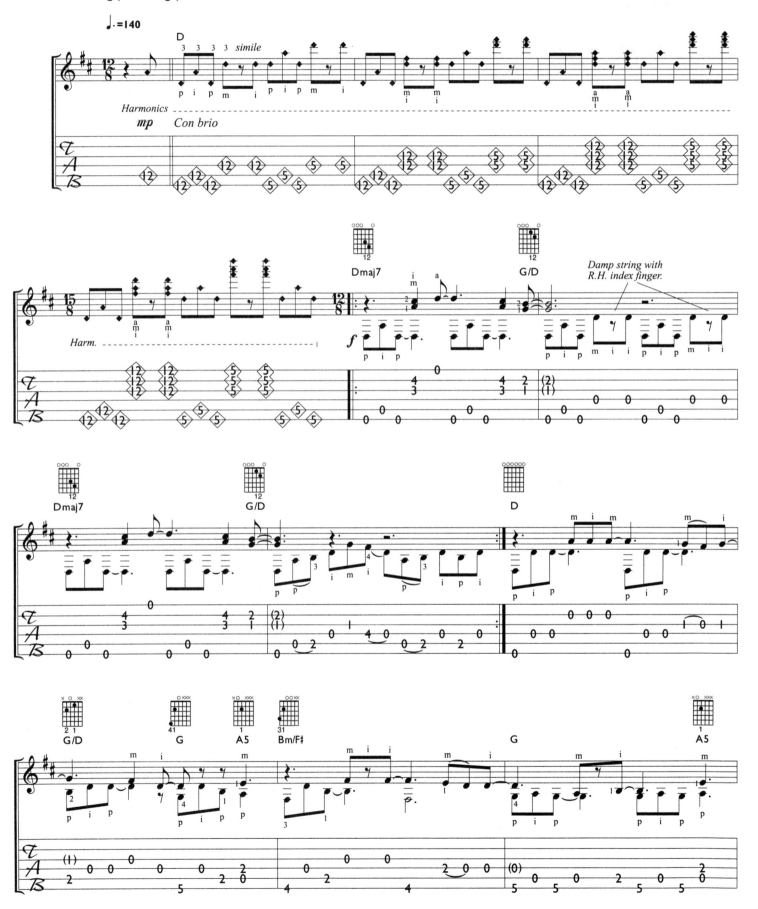

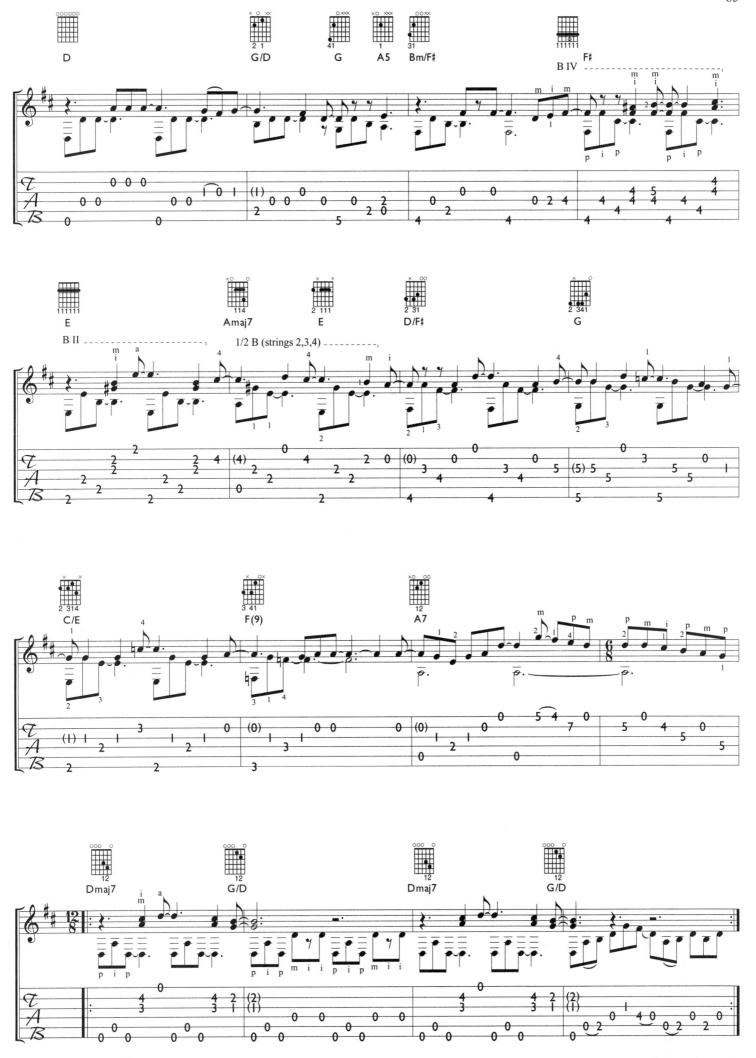

BELLA DONNA - 6 - 2

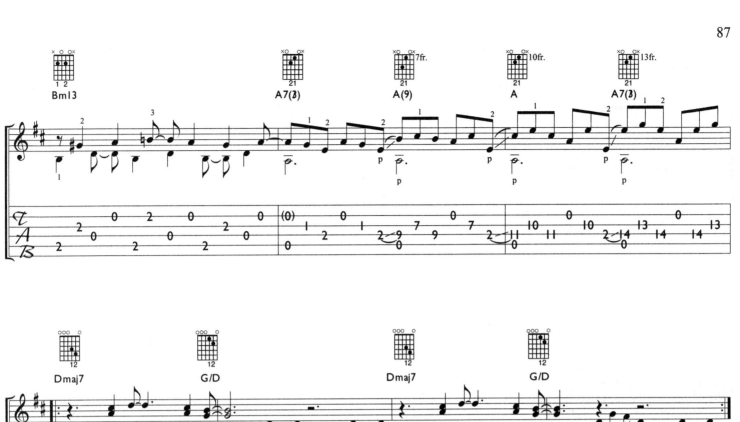

BELLA DONNA - 6 - 4

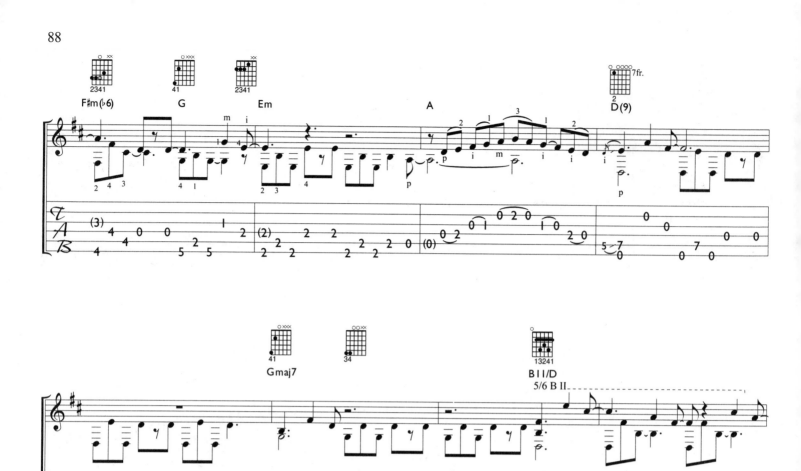

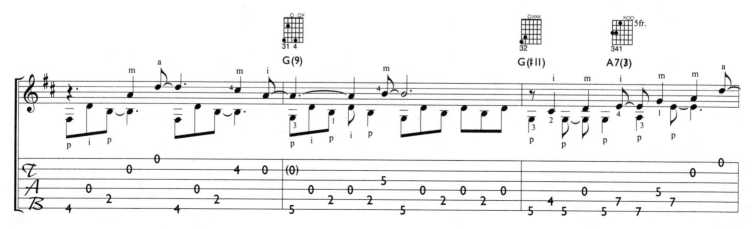

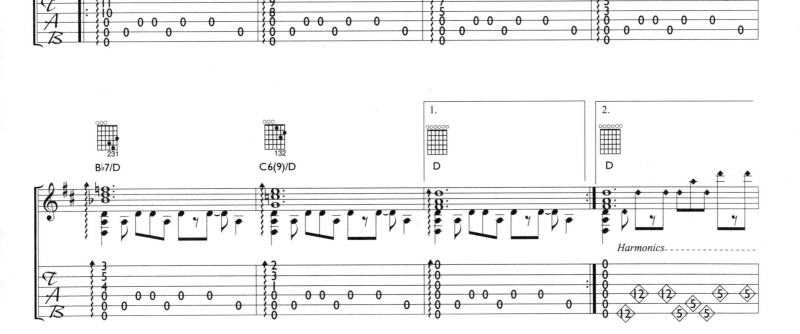

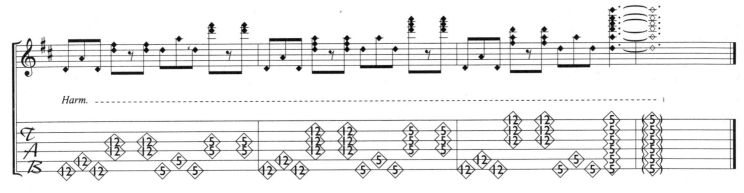

BELLA DONNA - 6 - 6

EBEGAD Tuning

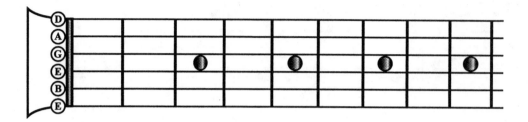

To change your tuning from standard to EBEGAD:

- Raise your 5th string a whole-step from A to B. The 7th fret on the 6th string (B) should now equal the 5th string open (B).

- Raise your 4th string a whole-step from D to E. The 4th string is now an octave above the 6th string low E. The 5th fret on the 5th string (E) should now equal the open 4th string (E).

- Lower your 2nd string a whole-step from B to A. The open 2nd string (A) should now equal the 3rd string, 2nd fret (A).

- Lower your 1st string a whole-step from E to D. The open 1st string (D) should now equal the 2nd string, 5th fret (D).

Play this simple etude to begin to familiarize yourself with the sound of this tuning. As you play this, notice how major and minor chords can be formed with simple barre chords.

EBEGAD Etude

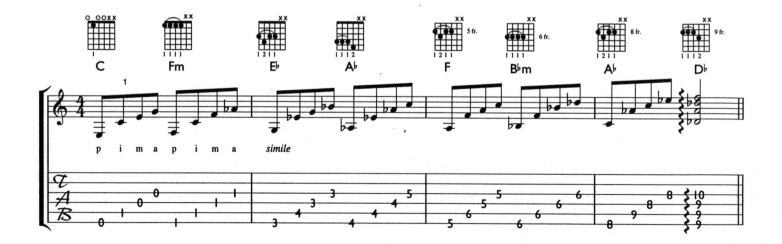

EBEGAD Tuning

Here is a nice sampling of chord voicings in EBEGAD tuning. Use these voicings to further familiarize yourself with this tuning and see what ideas they stimulate.

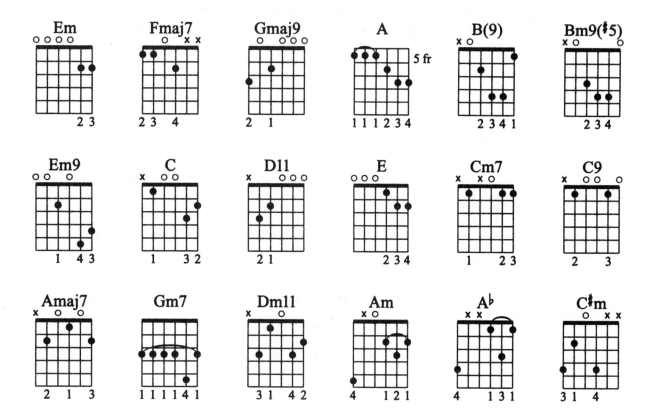

Here is my arrangement of a popular folk and bluegrass standard "Star of the County Down." Again, arranging familiar melodies in a new tuning is a good way to acquaint yourself with that tuning.

Star of County Down

Tuning (Low to high): EBEGAD

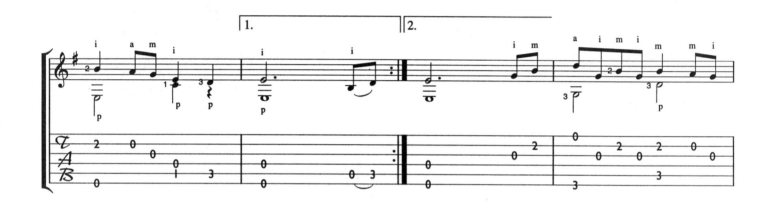

EBEGAD Performance Notes

Mother's Tears:

Very few things in life are more honest and heart-felt than a mother's tears of pain and joy. I tried to convey these feelings musically by modulating from the initial minor mode to the major mode in the closing part of the composition. This tune was inspired by the "Beguine" rhythm which is articulated by the bass notes.

Note 1: Measure 6

This natural harmonic is played by touching the 12th fret of the 1st string with the right hand index finger and simultaneously plucking the same string with the right hand ring finger. During this process you also have to sustain the chord played on the previous measure.

Note 2: Measure 12

The second beat of the measure is played with the right hand ring finger striking all six strings from down to up while holding the chord on the diagram. This effect is reminiscent of a cascade of notes created by a harp.

Mother's Tears

Peppino D'Agostino

MOTHER'S TEARS - 4 - 1

Damp 3rd string with L.H. little finger.

MOTHER'S TEARS - 4 - 2

Glossary Italian Terms

Affettuoso . . . . .Tender

Animando . . . . .Increasingly spirited

Appassionato . . . . .Passionate

Calmo . . . . .Calm

Cantabile . . . . .Melodious

Con brio . . . . .Vivacious

Con moto . . . . .With motion

Con tenerezza . . . . .Gently

Danzante . . . . .Suitable for dancing

Dolcissimo . . . . .Very sweet

Espressivo . . . . .Expressive

Maestoso . . . . .Majestic

Malinconico . . . . .Melancholic

Marcato . . . . .Strongly accented

Risoluto . . . . .Emphatically

Ritardando . . . . .Slowing down the tempo

Sereno . . . . .Serene

Vigoroso . . . . .Powerful

ACOUSTIC GUITAR TAB GLOSSARY

TABLATURE EXPLANATION

READING TABLATURE: Tablature illustrates the six strings of the guitar. Notes and chords are indicated by the placement of fret numbers on a given string(s).

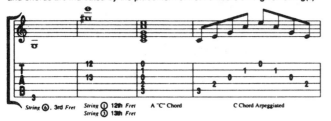

String ⑥, 3rd Fret   *String ① 12th Fret*   A "C" Chord   C Chord Arpeggiated
                String ③ 13th Fret

HARMONICS

NATURAL HARMONIC: A finger of the fret hand lightly touches the note or notes indicated in the tab and is played by the pick hand.

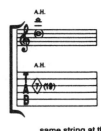

ARTIFICIAL HARMONIC: The first tab number is fretted, then the pick hand produces the harmonic by using a finger to lightly touch the same string at the second tab number (in parenthesis) and is then picked by another finger.

BENDING NOTES

HALF STEP: Play the note and bend string one half step.*

PREBEND (Ghost Bend): Bend to the specified note, before the string is picked.

WHOLE STEP: Play the note and bend string one whole step.

PREBEND AND RELEASE: Bend the string, play it, then release to the original note.

SLIGHT BEND (Microtone): Play the note and bend string slightly to the equivalent of half a fret.

BENDS INVOLVING MORE THAN ONE STRING: Play the note and bend string while playing an additional note (or notes) on another string(s). Upon release, relieve pressure from additional note(s), causing original note to sound alone.

DOUBLE NOTE BEND: Play both notes and immediately bend both strings simultaneously.

BENDS INVOLVING STATIONARY NOTES: Play notes and bend lower pitch, then hold until release begins (indicated at the point where line becomes solid).

ARTICULATIONS

HAMMER ON: Play lower note, then "hammer on" to higher note with another finger. Only the first note is attacked.

PULL OFF: Play higher note, then "pull off" to lower note with another finger. Only the first note is attacked.

LEFT HAND HAMMER: Hammer on the first note played on each string with the left hand.

MUTED STRINGS: A percussive sound is made by laying the fret hand across all six strings while pick hand strikes specified area (low, mid, high strings).

FRET-BOARD TAPPING: "Tap" onto the note indicated by + with a finger of the pick hand, then pull off to the following note held by the fret hand.